findin

I0628630

finding refuge

heart work for healing collective grief

MICHELLE CASSANDRA JOHNSON

SHAMBHALA

Shambhala Publications, Inc.
2129 13th Street
Boulder, Colorado 80302
www.shambhala.com

Cover art: Erin Robinson
Cover and interior design: Kate E. White

9 8 7 6 5 4 3 2 1

First Edition
Printed in the United States of America

♾ This edition is printed on acid-free paper that meets the
American National Standards Institute Z39.48 Standard.
♻ This book is printed on 30% postconsumer recycled paper.
For more information please visit www.shambhala.com.
Shambhala Publications is distributed worldwide by
Penguin Random House, Inc., and its subsidiaries.

LIBRARY OF CONGRESS CATALOGING-IN-PUBLICATION DATA
Names: Johnson, Michelle C., author.
Title: Finding refuge: heart work for healing collective grief /
Michelle Cassandra Johnson.
Description: First edition. | Boulder, Colorado: Shambhala, [2021] |
Includes bibliographical references.
Identifiers: LCCN 2020044448 | ISBN 9781611809367 (trade paperback)
Subjects: LCSH: Bereavement—Religious aspects. | Grief—
Religious aspects. | Suffering—Religious aspects.
Classification: LCC BL65.B47 J64 2021 | DDC 204/.42—dc23
LC record available at https://lccn.loc.gov/2020044448

This book is dedicated to my ancestors, known and unknown. Your ancestral wisdom is a force to be reckoned with and I am so grateful I am part of our powerful bloodline.

This book is dedicated to my mother, Clara. You are an everlasting light and constant inspiration for me. I love you dearly.

This book is dedicated to all who feel brokenhearted and are dedicated to making the world a place where we can find refuge amid all that breaks our hearts.

CONTENTS

FOREWORD

Grief does not change you ... It reveals you.

—JOHN GREEN, *The Fault in Our Stars*

I first met Michelle Cassandra Johnson when I wandered into a yoga studio where she taught in Carrboro, North Carolina. I was immediately taken. Her classes were a balm, a remembering, a calling-forth. She not only held space for us to center and resource ourselves from the deep well of our bodies, but unlike other yoga spaces I had been in, Michelle also called us up and out of ourselves and into the work of the world. She centered justice. She called us into the collective, not just the private inner world of our bodies on the mat. She reminded us that the internal was external, and vice versa. I knew immediately that I wanted to be friends with this powerful human being.

The more I learned about Michelle, the more I understood what a force she was. Everyone knew Michelle. Her spirit was big and her imprint was huge in our small town. She had an uncanny ability to call things into being. If Michelle decided to take something on—a project, a fundraiser, a campaign—it was as good as done. At some energetic level, when Michelle set an intention, it was as if deep tectonic plates started shifting and celestial winds started blowing.

Sometime shortly after we first met, I attended a Dismantling Racism workshop where Michelle was one of the trainers. Like her name, Cassandra, she is a seer and a drop-the-mic kind of truth-teller. She does not shy away from the truth, however painful. She does not look away from grief and trauma. And yet, masterfully, she is able to hold these spaces with grace, with great spaciousness, and with great kindness.

Over time, our friendship grew and deepened. We saw each other through marriages and divorces, and held one another in grief and joy. She officiated my husband's and my marriage ceremony and we became part of each other's chosen families. I watched my best friend fall apart after the death of Trayvon Martin and the acquittal of George Zimmerman. She held me through a brutal series of miscarriages. I was with her the night she found out her father had passed. We followed each other through moves across the country and began working together, co-facilitating anti-racism training in organizations. Michelle taught me more about friendship than I have ever known. She means it when she says to those she loves, with a twinkle in her eye, "Ride or die, boo. Ride or die."

To say that Michelle has changed my life is a paltry attempt at capturing the breadth and depth of that alchemy. To say she changes spaces and conducts energy in rooms is to watch a great artist, a great healer, at work.

When Michelle told me that she was writing a book on grief, we both knew it was not only something she would be channeling that the world needed to hear but it was also something she had been preparing for her whole life. As a Black woman in America, the lineage of grief pulses in her veins. So does a lineage of creativity, resilience, and joy. As a healer and intuitive, Michelle is called to work for the collective.

In this book, calling on the powerful metaphor of bees, Michelle writes:

> We are living during a time where it is important for us all to embrace the practice of collective care. We are living during a time where remembering we are precious to one another, and remembering that all parts of our ecosystem are precious to us, might allow us to heal the fragmentation that comes from living in a culture that doesn't allow us to be whole or see ourselves as part of the whole. . . . What would it be like for us to embody a responsibility for our collective hive? What would it be like to create spaces for us to grieve what has been lost as a result of our forgetting? That we are interconnected and part of a fragile and beautiful ecosystem, shared and composed of sentient beings whose survival is as important as our own? How might we begin to break down systems that separate us from remembering that we are part of a hive and that we have different roles to ensure our collective liberation and survival? What would it feel like to be devoted to the liberation of all?

Grief does not change us . . . it reveals us. What will our collective grief reveal? What can be transmuted if we move through our grief with great care for the collective, like the hive? Can the grief and trauma of racism, sexism, transphobia, and other systems of dominance transmute us if we allow ourselves to truly touch into that grief and hold one another through it? Can we repair across lines of power and privilege, offer reparations, attend to truth and reconciliation, and center love?

This is deep work and there are no easy answers. But Michelle Cassandra Johnson is an able guide for this journey. She extols us to breathe. To open our hearts. To allow ourselves to feel the heartbreak of a world bound in systems of oppression. She gives us practices, meditations, and mantras. Equal parts alchemist, seer, truth-teller, Michelle takes us on the journey of her own grief and guides us in lessons for how to transmute our own. Her words are a true embodiment of ahimsa, of service, and of love.

This book, like Michelle herself, is a great gift to the world.

—AMY BURTAINE,
co-author of *The Facilitator's Handbook for Leading White Racial Affinity Groups*

ACKNOWLEDGMENTS

First, I want to acknowledge my ancestors, in particular Dorothy, my maternal grandmother. My ancestors are responsible for my being. They are responsible for my work, and their support allows me to bring their dreams from the spiritual world into the material world. They shepherded me through a very difficult time that was filled with grief and loss because they knew I would land in a place where my spiritual practice could support me in responding to the grief that desperately needs to be felt and witnessed at this time. Thank you to the ancestors known to me and unknown. Thank you to the healthy ancestors who do their magic from the other side.

Speaking of magic, Charles Kurtz, my partner and twin flame, has done some magic to make my dreams come true too! We are opposites on the zodiac—he's an Aquarius and I am a Leo, and it is said that we are opposite sides of the same coin. Our union hasn't come easily, and our relationship has felt much of the grief written about in *Finding Refuge*. The points of tension in our relationship and the stars allowed me to deepen my love for myself and my spiritual practice. Our relationship has also been a refuge for me in so many ways. Charles has put together medicine bags, built fires, and talked with the bees and my grandmother, all in service of my magic. He has believed in my capacity to change the world since we first met. Charles, I appreciate your support, wizardry, and care as I try to do my part to heal the planet.

Thank you to Spirit, my altar, crystals, divination decks, journal, and spiritual tools. You gave me the fortitude to continue to write, breathe, be, and practice.

Thank you to the various goddess circles in my life. To my goddess circle in the Triangle area of North Carolina, I hold such deep reverence for our magic and hearts. You all have witnessed me through so much of what I have written about in *Finding Refuge*. We have sat in ceremony dreaming, crying, manifesting, chanting, praying, and drinking copious amounts of wine followed by consuming copious amounts of chocolate. When we first came together in my home four years ago, I had no idea the strength of our coven would be as immense as it is now. To my goddess circle in the Triad area of North Carolina, thank you for welcoming me to Winston-Salem and for being my people. You all have shown up for magic and ceremony, warming up my home and heart. You all have witnessed and trusted me, and we have been with each other through transition and change. You all have been cheerleaders for me, always wanting to see my dreams come true. Thank you.

To all the goddesses elsewhere in Seattle, California, Portland, and all over the world, thank you for being such a big part of my life. Some of you held me right after my father passed away. Some of you called me and sent money to support the patient advocate when my mom was sick. You all have sat in ceremony with me and seen me through some difficult and joyous times. Distance is just that, distance; our bond and love are ever present.

Thank you to my best friend, who might be my biggest cheerleader in the world. Amy, I love you to the moon and back. Always and forever.

Jeff, you have held some of the grief that is written about in *Finding Refuge*. You have seen it, listened to it, and validated that it was real. Thanks for being who you are—sweet, kind, and generous. Your spirit is so very generous.

Gratitude to the beloveds written about in *Finding Refuge*. Thank you, Clara, Cornelius, Emily, Eric, Dorothy, Sting, the Spice Girls, Infinity, Karla, and Mignon. You shaped the story. You have forever changed my life.

Thank you to Tristan Katz, who not only supported *Finding Refuge* into coming into being but also really wants my work and words to reach many. Thanks for being a collaborator, thought partner, friend, comrade, and teacher. I love you.

Thank you to Tatum Fjerstad. Tatum worked with me on my first book, *Skill in Action*. She believed in me as a person and writer and has cheered me on along the way. I love you, Tatum.

Thanks, Jasper. You are the sweetest and most devoted pup I have ever known. You've been on the journey with me every step of the way. I know you are a human who got stuck in a dog's body and I'm so very happy the dog version of you came into my life. You're pure medicine.

Lastly, I offer a deep bow of gratitude to my mother. Clara, you are a miracle. Truly. Thanks for being my mother. Thank you for being so much of the inspiration for *Finding Refuge*. Thank you for creating refuge in all the ways you have and do. You are everything, and I am so lucky that Spirit chose me to be your daughter in this lifetime.

finding refuge

INTRODUCTION

Turning toward My Own Grief

I remember the morning after.

I was in bed, unable to rise up and face the day. I had gone out to dinner with a friend the night before and had come home to the news that George Zimmerman had been acquitted for the murder of Trayvon Martin. I was standing in my kitchen, holding my phone, and I fell to the floor upon reading the news.

I don't remember all the details—trauma doesn't allow one to remember everything as it happens. I do remember the cold concrete floor, the sound of my wailing, and my heart, shattering in a way that felt irreparable. I felt dismembered, as if all the ancestral trauma of living in a Black body in a culture that doesn't value Blackness came out through tears, snot, and screams. I sat on the floor for what felt like hours, unable to stand up. My then-husband was rooms away. The depth of my despair overwhelmed our house and his nervous system, so he went to bed, leaving me to tend to the pieces of myself on the floor.

I was alone. I was afraid for myself. My Blackness felt more visible than ever. I couldn't go to bed—my own nervous system wouldn't allow it. This was a moment when everyone should have awakened. I wanted everyone to wake up to the reality that another innocent Black boy was murdered by a man, and his murder was justified by a criminal justice system backed by a white supremacist culture for standing his ground against Blackness.

I must have cried myself to sleep because I remember waking up the next morning with a grief hangover—puffy eyes, a hoarse voice, and utter exhaustion. My mind cloudy, my heart still broken. The grief for Trayvon and all the people whose hearts had contained hope prior to the verdict collided with my spirit like a tidal wave. I was flattened by this experience not only because the justice system made the choice to uphold injustice but also because I felt more like a target than ever before.

I called my clients to cancel sessions. I called a friend who understood I would never be the same person again. I stayed in bed, in deep sorrow and despair. I tried to sleep away what had just happened—another Black boy, gone, and a total lack of accountability for the person who murdered him. The grief in my bones was much larger than my body. It was the grief of my ancestors weeping for liberation, the grief of mothers preparing to birth Black babies, and the grief of a country that wanted to dissect Trayvon's character instead of mourn his life. I could not separate my grief from the grief and heartache Trayvon's mother must have felt. I couldn't separate it from a history of Black bodies being taken, murdered, disfigured, dismembered, lynched, and devalued.

At that moment, there was no way for me to separate my grief from all the losses Black people have endured due to white supremacy. I wanted everything to stop and for everyone to feel the gravity of what it meant to lose Trayvon—a Black child who had gone to the store to buy candy and never made it back home.

What happened instead was the world kept spinning and, while some felt deeply affected by the death of Trayvon and subsequent acquittal of George Zimmerman, others felt numb to the gravity of it all. I kept moving, even though my body wanted me to stop and take all the time I needed to heal. I kept moving because dominant culture—a system that inherently believes some people are superior and others are inferior based on various identities (e.g., race, gender, gender identity and expression, age, physical or mental capabilities, and sexual orientation)—had not created conditions for my grief to be experienced, felt, or seen. Dominant culture had not created conditions for my very being to be experienced, felt, or seen because it regards Blackness as something that should not exist. Dominant culture had decided I shouldn't grieve a Black body, and instead move forward as if Trayvon didn't mean anything. In reality, Trayvon meant everything.

The experience of not having space to grieve Trayvon mirrored the experience of what I learned to do in response to any loss: deny, pretend, lie, forget, be strong, and move forward. I learned how not to grieve from the media, my family, organizing and social justice circles, *and* dominant culture. I learned grief was processed behind closed doors or not at all. I learned to apologize for sadness as tears rolled down my cheeks. I learned the way to show strength is to show you can endure suffering. I learned to fight oppression without making space to honor the ways in which oppression was harming me and our social change movements.

Even if I wanted to tend to my grief over the loss of Trayvon and the history and impact of racism, white supremacy, and intergenerational trauma, I didn't have time. I had clients, a marriage, friends, and obligations that made it nearly impossible for me to carve out space to grieve. Plus, the heartbreak that I felt threatened to overwhelm my system. Heartbreak was always present. I did a good job of recognizing heartbreak but not mending it.

Prior to the acquittal of George Zimmerman, if my grief was severe enough and visible, people would tolerate it for a little while and then leave. After all, the pattern is that everyone comes to the funeral, brings food, and then leaves. Grief had been presented to me as a linear process to be moved through step-by-step; it was something to conquer, instead of a never-ending experience that feels as if it could knock one over with tidal-wave strength again and again. Institutions such as schools, nonprofits, and corporations have decided that three to five days is enough time for bereavement leave, making an assumption that it only takes that much time to mourn a loss. No one had taught me how to grieve because most people aren't taught how to make space for themselves to grieve. In my experience, white Western culture is unsure about how to give attention to grief and loss. And when there is a focus on grief, it is usually focused on an individual's loss—not the loss we are experiencing as a culture and collective.

While I navigated my life with a broken heart, all I wanted was quiet and solitude. The borders of the world felt like they were closing in on me. The world didn't make sense to me. My medicine came through my commitment to spiritual practice. While I tried to find stillness in meditation, it was difficult to deny my grief. My brain tried to bypass it; my breath coaxed me into feeling it. Once I began to feel the breath and heartache, I began to feel my sorrow surface and flow through.

After Trayvon, lives continued to be taken by white supremacy and my heart continued to break, cracking open to reveal my capacity to hold heartache and be a catalyst for social change. Not only was my heart's capacity to hold heartache revealed to me but the nature of my work also shifted. I went from holding space as a therapist, yoga teacher, elected official, and Dismantling Racism trainer for individuals moving through grief to a person who understood what was being experienced by individuals wasn't isolated, and instead, was a collective experience. This lens of collective grief transformed my work, and I became focused on collective grief and healing justice. Trayvon's murder and the acquittal of George Zimmerman changed the trajectory of my life.

In my spiritual practice and social change work, I had to learn how to grieve and name heartbreak. I had to resource myself and others by remembering the power of spiritual practice: prayer, ritual, meditation, ceremony, yoga, breathing, mindfulness, and movement. My spiritual practice taught me to be present to my grief. The practice of presence and attending to my grief allowed me to begin picking up the shattered parts of myself and piecing them back together. My spiritual practice allowed me to expose unprocessed grief, thus allowing healing to happen.

I know many are feeling shattered and in pieces at this time. Not just in response to the loss of Trayvon and so many others, or how many people with less proximity to power are devalued, but also in response to all that feels overwhelming at this time in our country and world. We are holding grief in our bodies and bones, often in isolation. And yet, our grief isn't isolated. It is pervasive.

To respond to the grief that we experience as a collective, we need to be present to what is breaking our hearts. We need a spiritual practice to hold and allow us to feel grounded as we begin to recognize our brokenheartedness. When we turn toward our brokenheartedness, I believe we can begin to acknowledge what we are grieving, and we can create space to grieve. As we grieve, we also tap into our own capacity to heal. We connect with our resilience and begin to piece back together the parts of ourselves that feel shattered. We come back into wholeness.

Finding Refuge is a book designed to guide you through exploring what is breaking your heart, where grief resides, and how it affects you. This book is intended to serve as a tool for healing yourself, thus allowing you to create conditions to heal what continually shatters many of us—the immense amount of suffering on the planet. It is a resource designed for you to be present with your grief by committing to a spiritual practice. And, it is a resource designed for you to digest the unprocessed grief that has emerged from the losses we are experiencing as a collective—the planet, resources, relationships, connection, and the pain of living in an unjust world. It is a resource that beckons you to be present to your brokenheartedness while remaining openhearted.

As you engage with the content in this book, know that each one of us has a role to play in building enough momentum to shift what is so wrong in this spinning world. *Finding Refuge* is an invitation to intentionally move through a journey focused on remembering your wholeness and divinity by engaging spiritual practice, meditation, reflection, movement, breathing, ritual, journaling, and connecting with others to stay grounded and take action with an open heart during heartbreaking times. To prepare for this journey, I invite you to do the following:

1. Review the shared language section and assumptions to familiarize yourself with the language presented in *Finding Refuge*.
2. As you explore spiritual practice, get a private journal for recording reflections and staying grounded during uncertain

times. This journal will serve as a space for you to record your thoughts, feelings, awakenings, and ideas.

3. Create a space in your home, car, office, or a natural landscape (such as a favorite park, hillside, a river, or stream) to practice the meditations and breath practices offered throughout the book. It's simple. You don't need a yoga mat or any props; you just need a space where you can breathe, sit, tune in to your intuition and highest self, and allow yourself to just be.

4. Lastly, I encourage you to find an object that represents what is breaking your heart at this time. Choose an object that is meaningful to you—an object that represents your heart's capacity to be open and acknowledge heartbreak. Place this object in a location where you will see it daily to remind you of the importance of acknowledging your heart and giving your heartbreak the attention it needs to heal individually and aid in healing the collective.

SHARED LANGUAGE

Language is a powerful tool. The way one uses language can shape and shift culture. In *Finding Refuge*, I use terminology that may be new to you or may be used in a different way than you are accustomed to. It is important to have a shared understanding of language as one explores the concepts of cultural trauma, systemic oppression, and collective grief. Many of the definitions offered here are informed by my work with Dismantling Racism Works (dRworks—a training collective focused on dismantling racism in communities and organizations), my book *Skill in Action*, critical race and feminist theory, as well as scholars who have been studying and exploring oppression for the whole of their lives.

CULTURE

Norms, standards, beliefs, values, and narratives that are created by a particular nation, people, or social group.

DOMINANT CULTURE

Dominant culture is a system that inherently believes some people are superior and others inferior. This system of dominance and inferiority is based on various identities such as race, gender, gender identity and expression, age, physical or mental capabilities, and sexual orientation. Dominant culture creates norms, thus deeming who is "normal." When one is seen as normal based on their identities, this gives them closer proximity to power. Therefore, dominant culture functions as a gatekeeper by deciding who has access to power and access to moving with ease as they navigate their life.

SOCIAL LOCATION

Social location refers to social group membership and identities. It is a tool used to reflect on the groups that people belong to because of their place or position in history and society. It is a tool used to allow people to clearly identify their proximity to power based on identities they embody. Everyone has a social location that is defined by race, gender, gender expression, social class, age, ability level, sexual orientation, geographic location, and context.

CISGENDER

One is cisgender when their gender identity matches their assigned sex at birth.

INTERSECTIONALITY

A term coined by Kimberlé Crenshaw and first spoken of by Sojourner Truth, intersectionality asks us to consider all the identities we embody—the ones that are assigned privilege and the ones that experience oppression—due to the culture's construction of identities and the value or lack of value it places on these identities. Intersectionality asks us to look at the intersection of our identities to better understand how we navigate the world and how we work across lines of difference. For example, I am a Black, able-bodied, middle-class, heterosexual, cisgender woman.

TRAUMA

There are many types of trauma. For the purposes of understanding trauma within the context of *Finding Refuge*, I define it as a disruption of and shock to the nervous system and an experience that causes one or a group of people to move out of balance. It is often an experience that is not within one's control. Often, one has to engage healing modalities such as therapy, movement, energy work, journaling, yoga, pranayama, meditation, ceremony, and ritual to bring the nervous system back into homeostasis.

CULTURAL TRAUMA

Dysregulation of the collective's nervous system, often due to systemic oppression and in response to tragic and horrific events that forever shift a group of people's consciousness and identity. Cultural trauma acknowledges the shared experience of trauma even as people respond to the traumatic event(s) differently.

COLLECTIVE GRIEF

Grief felt by the collective in response to loss that affects us all such as war, a pandemic, oppressive policies, historical trauma, and systemic oppression.

OPPRESSION

Oppression is the subjugation of one group of people to elevate another group of people. Often, it involves violence, but oppression isn't limited to physical violence. It can include emotional, mental, spiritual, and psychic violence as well.

PRIVILEGE

Privilege is the societal benefit bestowed upon people socially, politically, and economically. Privilege can be based on race, class, age, ability level, mental health status, gender identity, and sex.

WHITE SUPREMACY

The idea (ideology) that white people and the ideas, thoughts, beliefs, and actions of white people are superior to People of Color and their ideas, thoughts, beliefs, and actions. While most people associate white supremacy with extremist groups such as the Ku Klux Klan and the neo-Nazis, white supremacy is ever present in our institutional and cultural assumptions that assign value, morality, goodness, and humanity to the white group while casting people and communities of color as worthless (worth less), immoral, bad, inhuman, and "undeserving." Drawing from critical race theory, the term *white supremacy* also refers to a political or socioeconomic system where white people enjoy structural advantage and rights that other racial and ethnic groups do not, both at a collective and an individual level.

RACISM

Racism is racial prejudice + social and institutional power.
Racism is advantage based on race.
Racism is oppression based on race.
Racism is a white supremacy system.

SUFFERING

In many religious or faith traditions, understanding the afflictions that cause suffering inspires deeper exploration of how we create a space of ultimate liberation and freedom. Given the historical legacy of war, violence, oppression, socially and politically constructed categories used to minimize people and make them be seen as subhuman, and the privileging of groups of people at the expense of others, it is important to broaden the definition of suffering to move beyond the individual. Social and political forces have caused collective pain and cultural trauma. These forces have normalized things that are absolutely absurd, such as the number of children who go to bed hungry at night or the amount of Black and Brown bodies that are murdered at the hands of police who are supported by a criminal justice system that chooses to serve and protect some and annihilate others. Suffering is the experience of pain and distress psychically, emotionally, physically, mentally, and spiritually.

SPIRITUAL BYPASSING

Spiritual bypassing is a term coined by John Welwood. He defined spiritual bypassing as "spiritual ideas and practices to sidestep personal, emotional 'unfinished business,' to shore up a shaky sense of self, or to belittle basic needs, feelings, and developmental tasks."* I offer his definition here because many of the practices I created for healing in *Finding Refuge* call us into working with Spirit and our embodied divinity. The practices in the book are for healing and not intended for one to avoid what truly needs healing. Spiritual bypassing arises in many spiritual spaces, which causes great harm to us all.

* Diana Raab, "What Is Spiritual Bypassing," *Psychology Today*, January 23, 2019, https://www.psychologytoday.com/us/blog/the-empowerment-diary /201901/what-is-spiritual-bypassing.

An example of this is the use of the phrase "We are one." This belief is a tenant of many spiritual practices and religions and is an absolute truth. And yet, we live in a culture where we are not able to live as one due to systemic oppression. We are not having the same experience based on our different identities, social locations, and proximities to power. A valuable practice is being able to hold an absolute truth while holding the reality of what is happening that moves us away from that truth. We cannot bypass grief and trauma—we must move through our grief and trauma to heal. Spiritual practice is designed for us to see things as they are, which means we must see, sense, and feel collective suffering, understand how we might be perpetuating suffering, recognize when we stay silent when we know the causes of suffering, and work to break toxic patterns to truly heal.

LIBERATION

As with the definition of suffering, many religious and faith traditions focus on the pathway to enlightenment, freeing ourselves of our attachments to afflictions (our own suffering), and shifting our consciousness such that we can be free, regardless of the circumstances. In *Man's Search for Meaning*, Viktor Frankl discusses the space between what was happening to him when he was in a concentration camp and what was within his power to change under these conditions. He describes the physical and psychological experience, and his response was, "Between stimulus and response there is a space. In that space is our power to choose our response. In our response lies our growth and our freedom." Viktor Frankl is correct: from a psychic perspective, our freedom does live between what is happening to us, the stimulus, and our response. Liberation is understanding our humanity and being able to see the humanity in others such that we understand our freedom is dependent upon others' freedom.

"OPPRESSION TAKES THE BREATH AWAY"

This is a phrase I first used in July 2014, after the murder of Eric Garner. I watched the video of his murder, went to teach a noon yoga class, and spoke these words for the first time: *We live in a culture where oppression takes the breath away*. It does so physically by taking away someone's capacity to breathe; emotionally by causing great suffering through the act of oppression and subjugation; mentally by causing anxiety, post-traumatic stress disorder (PTSD), depression, and grief; and spiritually by trying to extinguish one's life force. *Finding Refuge* explores the grief we experience in response to the fact that oppression takes the breath away.

LIVING ANCESTOR

This is a concept first introduced to me by Layla Saad, the author of *Me and White Supremacy*. Layla hosts a podcast called *Good Ancestor* where she explores what it means to be a good ancestor with her guests. The premise is that we are supported by our ancestors who have transitioned, and we are living ancestors, deciding what our legacy will be with our actions, intentions, beliefs, and how we express our values and what we value.

My friend and colleague, Stephanie Ghoston Paul, has also created a podcast called *Take Nothing When I Die*, which is an exploration of what it means to be a living ancestor. Stephanie focuses on the dreams we can manifest, the words we can say, and the actions we can take now instead of taking them to the graveyard with us after we transition. So many people's dreams, inventions, wishes, hopes, and desires live in the graveyard or wherever you believe one goes after they leave their physical body. Being a living ancestor is about bringing our dreams, inventions, wishes, hopes, and desires to fruition now so we and future generations can benefit from them.

SPIRIT

I conceptualize "Spirit" as a power and energy that is much larger than me and contained inside me. Spirit can be felt through the elements—air, water, on the earth, in the heavens, in our bodies, and around us. People use different words to describe Spirit, including God, Father, Divine Mother, Creator, and so on. Spirit is an energy who I seek guidance and support from. I pray to Spirit and my spirit guides each day. Spirit guides are energies in the spiritual, not the material world, who are positive in nature and offer assistance to me in various ways. Spirit guides are sometimes referred to as angels, archangels, guardians, elemental energies, and ancestors.

APPROACH AND ASSUMPTIONS

It's important to be clear about my perspective and to communicate it with others as I engage in the work of uncovering, holding, and stewarding grief. Some of these assumptions derive from a collaboration with my colleagues at dRworks. Some are based on my evolution as a yoga teacher, activist, social worker, Dismantling Racism trainer, steward of grief, and space holder:

- Cultural trauma affects us all. Cultural trauma often derives from the toxicity that manifests from dominant culture and systems of superiority. Many of us are not encouraged to see the toxic culture or to grieve in response to it. Our practice of grieving collectively is a way of honoring our cultural trauma.

- Making space to acknowledge and honor our collective grief isn't a new practice. Many cultures have engaged in rituals focused on collective grief. Dominant culture has made some of us forget our lineages, rituals, and practices centered around grief. To heal, we must grieve what we have lost due to systems of oppression, the horrific nature of dominant culture, and the suffering it creates for us all.

- Intention is not the same as impact. We need to understand that we can have good intentions and still have a hurtful or damaging impact.

- We have different identities and lived experiences. It is important for us to be aware of our points of privilege and oppression as we make space to grieve. Grief does not land in the same way for everyone. Often, our points of privilege and oppression, plus our proximities to power, define our relationship with losses that are experienced due to systemic oppression.

- There isn't one way to grieve. The tools offered in *Finding Refuge* are just some of the tools one can engage to move through personal and collective grief. Often, the process of grieving isn't linear, and the way you choose to grieve may not make sense to others.

- Spiritual practice is one way we can move through grief. Spiritual practice invites us to cultivate our awareness of the causes of suffering and how we might be perpetuating suffering, and asks us to contemplate what conditions need to be in place for our collective liberation. Spiritual practice urges us to transform and make change for the collective good.

- We have to develop awareness of ourselves, our communities, and of the world, both as individuals and in community; we have to work together to love ourselves into who we want to be.
- The deep work of acknowledging the collective losses we have experienced isn't easy work. It is work we must do anyway. We must do this work to heal individually and collectively.

A BRAVE AND STARTLING TRUTH

We, this people, on a small and lonely planet
Traveling through casual space
Past aloof stars, across the way of indifferent suns
To a destination where all signs tell us
It is possible and imperative that we learn
A brave and startling truth

And when we come to it
To the day of peacemaking
When we release our fingers
From fists of hostility
And allow the pure air to cool our palms

When we come to it
When the curtain falls on the minstrel show of hate
And faces sooted with scorn are scrubbed clean
When battlefields and coliseum
No longer take our unique and particular sons and
    daughters
Up with the bruised and bloody grass
To lie in identical plots in foreign soil

When the rapacious storming of the churches
The screaming racket in the temples have ceased
When the pennants are waving gaily
When the banners of the world tremble
Stoutly in the good, clean breeze

When we come to it
When we let the rifles fall from our shoulders
And children dress their dolls in flags of truce
When land mines of death have been removed
And the aged can walk into evenings of peace
When religious ritual is not perfumed
By the incense of burning flesh
And childhood dreams are not kicked awake
By nightmares of abuse

When we come to it
Then we will confess that not the Pyramids
With their stones set in mysterious perfection
Nor the Gardens of Babylon
Hanging as eternal beauty
In our collective memory
Not the Grand Canyon
Kindled into delicious color
By Western sunsets

Nor the Danube, flowing its blue soul into Europe
Not the sacred peak of Mount Fuji
Stretching to the Rising Sun
Neither Father Amazon nor Mother Mississippi
        who, without favor,
Nurture all creatures in the depths and on the shores
These are not the only wonders of the world

When we come to it
We, this people, on this minuscule and kithless globe

Who reach daily for the bomb, the blade and the dagger
Yet who petition in the dark for tokens of peace
We, this people on this mote of matter
In whose mouths abide cankerous words
Which challenge our very existence
Yet out of those same mouths
Come songs of such exquisite sweetness
That the heart falters in its labor
And the body is quieted into awe

We, this people, on this small and drifting planet
Whose hands can strike with such abandon
That in a twinkling, life is sapped from the living
Yet those same hands can touch with such healing,
    irresistible tenderness
That the haughty neck is happy to bow
And the proud back is glad to bend
Out of such chaos, of such contradiction
We learn that we are neither devils nor divines

When we come to it
We, this people, on this wayward, floating body
Created on this earth, of this earth
Have the power to fashion for this earth
A climate where every man and every woman
Can live freely without sanctimonious piety
Without crippling fear

When we come to it
We must confess that we are the possible

We are the miraculous, the true wonder of this world
That is when, and only when
We come to it.

—MAYA ANGELOU

Roots are not in a landscape, or a country, or a people; they're usually inside yourself.

—Isabel Allende

THE ROOT

I pulled up an image of lavender-blue on my phone to make sure I had the exact color she spoke of. She nodded her head, pointed to the phone, and put her index finger on the screen. She seemed pleased that I was able to find such a beautiful shade of lavender-blue. I was trying to decipher what she meant when she said "lavender-blue and cinnamon." I wondered if she was perhaps telling me what color she wanted to be buried in while also remembering the cinnamon color of the bridesmaids' dresses from my wedding. Or maybe she was remembering the lavender-blue hydrangeas that lived in my grandmother's back-yard and the ones that surprised me in my backyard when I purchased my home in Winston-Salem. She lay there in a hospital bed, confused, affirming that she felt like she was underwater.

Sometimes, I feel underwater when I fly, changing altitude and time zones. Or when I haven't slept, which has been a chronic problem since childbirth. My experiences of being submerged are tame in comparison to what my mother was feeling. She felt like she was drowning, and I believed that might actually happen. My mother had lost thirty pounds, refused to eat or drink, and seemed to be leaving her physical body and moving on to another realm.

She had spent ten weeks in beds that weren't her own, in hospitals and skilled nursing facilities that didn't feel like home, receiving a lack of care and compassion from the system of "health care." My mother had entered the hospital on April 5, two days after I went to visit her for a belated birthday celebration. On my drive back to Richmond, this time to visit her in the hospital, many thoughts raced through my mind.

The doctors had started to run tests on my mother, and I knew she was experiencing the medical system as she and I always have, as a place where our wisdom about our own bodies is dismissed. For over a decade prior to this hospitalization, doctors had given my mother cortisone shots in her knees, put stockings on her to move lymph through her body and flush her system, administered breathing tests because of her asthma, poked and prodded her, all the while doubting her when she would say, "No, I don't have diabetes." Because the assumption, if you are an overweight Black woman, is that you must have terrible eating habits and have diabetes. My heart felt my mother's and I knew she was re-experiencing what it is like to be treated as a subject instead of a human being.

After her first week in the first hospital, the doctor, who was white, had come into the room and my mother had said, "Give me the bad news first."

The doctor had started to laugh, not recognizing the power he embodied—he was there to tell my mother what was "wrong" with her. He had the medical degree and he controlled how many tests were to be done on my mother's body, as well as when she would be discharged from the hospital.

He said, "We think you have a pinched nerve, and we want to discharge you to a skilled nursing facility to receive physical and occupational therapy."

My mom looked confused. I piped up and said, "How is she going to do therapy when she cannot sit up? She screams in excruciating pain whenever someone comes in to adjust her bed from horizontal toward vertical. She cannot move, walk, or sit up. How are you going to discharge her now?"

While I'd appreciated the doctor pulling up a chair and having very good bedside manner, I was angry—not just for my mother, but for all the people who are seen as bodies that are not valued in this culture.

He then asked, "Oh, she cannot sit up?" He should have known this fact. Her body had been in the hospital for six days—with him as her doctor *for all six of those days*.

Trying to keep my cool and stay centered while encountering and challenging a doctor who has been trained in a medical institution to believe he is all-knowing and conditioned by a world that values his whiteness over my mother's wellness, I angrily stated, "No, she cannot sit up." If I hadn't been in the room, I am certain my mother would have been discharged. Diagnosis: pinched nerve. Treatment: physical and occupational therapy.

The doctor reluctantly ordered two more tests: an X-ray of her spine and an MRI of her brain. Had he not run those tests, he would not have discovered that my mother had cervical spinal stenosis causing the pinched nerve and an infection in her lumbar spine. Her spine, at the top and bottom, were literally out of alignment and inflamed.

I couldn't help but see the parallel between my mother's illness and the sickness that dominant culture perpetuates. My mother had an infection in her spine—at the root of her spine. My mother's vertebrae were not only inflamed and infected but there was also minimal cartilage between them. Her spine was compressed, making it more difficult for her to stand or sit upright and tall. While my mother and I were challenged by dominant culture through the system of "health care" at every turn, I kept considering the infection dominant culture has at the root, never allowing us to physically or psychically stand upright and tall in our humanity.

Almost three months later, after my mother's illness had continued through three hospitals and three skilled nursing facilities, I sat with her in the third hospital as she struggled to express feelings through words. When she couldn't, she tried to write them down, producing squiggly lines that left her worried about herself and me heartbroken. She could tell she had become progressively confused. Her lack of lucidity coupled with her deteriorating body made her mostly pleasant and docile. The nurses kept commenting on how "cute" she was. I just sat back and thought, "She's a seventy-six-year-old woman. Children are cute. My mother is sick and looks near death. Nothing about this situation is 'cute.'" By the time my mom was taken to Virginia Commonwealth University Hospital, she was being given fluids by IV and she wasn't eating. She refused to nourish her body. She told me she was dying and said, "It won't be long, now."

When I was born, the afterbirth emerged before I did, causing the doctors and nurses to pull me out rather forcefully into this brutal and beautiful world. They moved me to a different hospital, away from my mother, for nine days. I was placed in an incubator while my 2 lb. 3 oz. body tried to sustain life. And now I watched my mother approaching death, in that same hospital.

At times, my breath was taken away by this reality. How did I end up in the same hospital as the one I had been in as a baby, fighting for my life, now watching my mother's health decline? I sat with her, and while I didn't support her not eating or drinking, I also didn't support giving her a feeding tube. I understood my mother. Her body was tired, her heart dispirited, and she trusted that she was going to be with my grandmother, Dorothy, who had transitioned just a year and a half before.

She told me she had been talking to my grandmother and others. My mother talking with Spirit and the ancestors calmed me. I was glad she didn't feel alone. It was difficult for my mother to communicate with those of us trying to offer her support in the physical realm, and I was glad she could find support in the ethereal realm. As she spoke with our ancestors and Spirit, I knew a decision was being made about whether it was time to stay here in her physical body or move beyond her body into the fullness of her spirit.

Throughout this experience, I witnessed various people in white coats and scrubs moving around medical institutions without any awareness of their own spirits, bodies, and hearts. I watched heartless behavior, like the skilled nursing facility staff overmedicating my mother to the point of her being unable to speak, know where she was, or what was going on around her. The same skilled nursing facility staff who didn't give my mother her IV antibiotics when she first arrived and couldn't be bothered with my request that turned into a demand to give my mother her medicine. One nurse explained how busy they were and that they were waiting on the pharmacy. I said to them, "This is my mother. She is precious to me. She needs her medicine." I was angry because I knew that I should not have had to remind someone working in a system meant to heal us that my mother's life was precious. I also knew the system of health care wasn't designed for health—it is designed to treat symptomatic people, but only if dominant culture deems them worthy enough to live.

The disregard of my concerns and my mother's needs occurred because of what white supremacy and oppression strip away from us: our ability to connect to ourselves and recognize our own humanity and divinity—the divinity that each one of us embodies. This is a divinity we embody even as we are encouraged to lose our connection with other sentient beings. When one loses connection with oneself, it is difficult to see the humanity in others. It is a challenge to digest and process the grief that arises from being severed from our collective innate divinity, humanity, and wholeness. It becomes impossible to interrupt patterns of violence, loss, dominance, and harm—behaviors that led to my mother being uncared for.

I sat in the space of watching my familial root—my mother—face death as my country played a game of risk with humanity itself through oppressive policies and practices, horrific violence, and cultural genocide. The trauma of watching my mother's body and the institution of medicine fail her, coupled with seeing our spinning world at war, the uninterrupted pattern of Black and Brown bodies and souls murdered, women being stripped of the power to have control over their bodies, and a president who seems to have a death wish for us all—well, those of us who aren't cis, white, straight, and male citizens—overwhelmed my system. The heartbreak from the trauma of watching a body with an inflamed root, while living in a country with an infection at its root at the base of how we came to be challenged my capacity to remain openhearted and induced a conjuring of the deepest expression of my spiritual practice thus far.

Deeper than anything I'd ever known.

The moment my mother had known she couldn't move, she had pushed her medical monitor button; she had asked for help because she had known something was terribly wrong and that she deserved care. She had acknowledged her need for care in the face of a total lack of care from previous doctors, nurses, and home health aides. My mother had experienced racism before. Not being cared for by institutions whose missions were to care for people wasn't new for her. As her illness progressed, she had tried to advocate for herself—asking the doctor questions and saying no to more tests and X-rays when her body had become tired.

During the first few weeks of her illness, she had felt strong enough to fight. Trying to get someone's attention from the nurses' station because she needed medicine, she had thrown a food tray across the room. She got her medicine after being pushed to act out of character because no one was listening to what she needed. She knew what she was facing, but as her illness progressed, her mind declined, and it became harder for her to fight and to connect with her will to live. I believe she was exercising the only agency she had left when she stopped eating and drinking; she would control how she went from this world and left her body—she wouldn't let anyone force her to stay alive by feeding her food through a tube and giving her liquids through an IV. She would decide the outcome. She had known I was by her side and advocating for her as best I could in a system that wasn't designed to listen to me, either—my Blackness, like hers, was perceived as a threat to white institutions.

While my mother, the ancestors, and Spirit were contemplating whether she would stay in a physical body, I was absorbing the trauma of watching my mother wither away. As I watched, the potential loss of her was always present even though I knew I would lose her one day. Spiritual practice had taught me that everything was temporary. The reality of the temporary nature of things wasn't what felt untenable. It was witnessing my mother not being cared for that was untenable. Even as her body began to fail her, the health-care system was not putting conditions in place for her to die with dignity. My grief in response to watching this process of dehumanization was immense. The lack of care we received was made invisible by systems that were never designed to hold our sickness, humanity, liberation, or grief.

I know trauma took up residence in my bones because, months later, whenever someone would ask about my mother, I would feel an automatic welling up of tears in my eyes. During the time when my mother was ill, I had to make decisions about her care, give updates to family members and my mother's friends, and attend to my mom, who was out of her mind most of the time. I didn't get to be her daughter. I became her caregiver. And in caregiver mode, I could acknowledge what was happening, the truth of what we were facing: the substandard care in these hospitals and skilled nursing facilities might have caused my mother to die, which presented another trauma to which I had to respond. My mother was just a body to the "health-care" system, not a human or someone's mother.

I knew my mother wasn't the only person facing institutional and cultural racism. I knew she wouldn't be the last person to be mistreated by systems designed to oppress her. I knew the people who worked in those systems were trained not to attach to patients, but instead to dissociate from their own humanity and the humanity of the people they were tasked with caring for.

One day as I sat in the hospital, sure that my mother would be transitioning very soon, I witnessed myself feeling heartbroken and calm. I could feel my heartbreak and I could sit and be fully present with my mother. None of what was happening felt easy, but I was in a place of acceptance. I don't know if it was from sheer exhaustion, or from handing what was happening over to Spirit and my ancestors, or from years of spiritual practice. Maybe all three. I sat with my mother, and I took a deep breath. Resourcing myself, I prayed, and I gazed at my mother and made a request of Spirit and of my grandmother. I accepted that my mother might leave her physical body and I requested that her transition be filled with ease. I knew the essence of who she was would live on forever.

My spiritual practice allowed me to sit with heartbreak and open my heart enough not to hold on to my mother, not to need her to stay in her physical body. I knew her spirit was much bigger than her body and, perhaps in that moment, healing looked like no longer creating conditions for her continued suffering.

Although all signs pointed to my mother dying, she conferred with the ancestors in community and chose to stay for a little bit longer. My mother didn't die. Instead, she made an almost full recovery. She worked hard to heal in the face of institutional and cultural racism and trauma and, once she knew it was possible to heal, she fought to get back home.

Through it all, and with a broken and open heart, I remained connected with my own heart, and with my mother's heart. I felt my heart ache. I felt the weight of the world and the ways we as a people try to break each other as a result of being disconnected from our hearts and, at times, are unwilling to see how that disconnection leads to suffering, individually and collectively. A connection with the heartache and grief that comes from watching a system repeatedly take away someone's humanity by treating them less than human is what will allow us to see how dominant culture works hard to break us.

If we desire wholeness amid dominant culture's striving to continually fragment us, we must deepen our connection with our hearts. If we desire to heal ourselves and create conditions for others to heal, we must grieve our heartache. We must remember that we are whole even when our hearts are broken. A deeper connection with the heart—both what causes it to feel pain and grieve, and find ease and heal—is necessary at this time.

One pathway to deepening your connection with your heart is to begin to feel what is present there.

PRACTICE
Being Present with My Heart

For this practice, you will need your journal and the object you have chosen to use for your journey through *Finding Refuge*. This practice invites you to connect with your heart. As you engage with this practice, you may want to be mindful of how triggering it can be to focus on what is present in the heart, given that it is one of the most vulnerable organs we embody, physically and energetically. Be tender with yourself and know this is a practice you can revisit time and time again.

We will start with a breathing practice to quiet your mind.

Find a comfortable seat, or if you prefer, you can stand or lie down. Place your object next to you or near you. You might want to elevate your hips by sitting on a cushion, pillow, or blanket.

Close your eyes, or gaze softly at the ground in front of you, and begin to breathe into your body. Start by taking deep breaths in and out. Begin to feel the shape change in your body as you breathe in and out. Notice the expansion as you breathe in and the contraction or release with your exhale.

Now, continue to breathe and begin to match the length of your inhale and exhale. This equal-part breathing can help with clarity and quieting the mind.

Sit for at least three minutes practicing equal-part breathing.

Notice the physical sensations and the emotions.

Bring your awareness to the object and notice your connection with it and the energy it is offering to you now.

Each of our hearts is being affected by these utterly overwhelming times. We are affected in different ways based on our identities—privileged and marginalized, visible and invisible.

Bring your awareness to your heart and consider what you are holding in your heart. This may be something very personal or something related to what is happening in the collective. When my mother was sick, I was attuned to both the pain of potentially losing a parent and the injustice of my mother not being cared for as a result of systemic oppression. Your heart may be holding something related to your marginalized identities and dominant culture's attempts to deny you the right to liberation. Or because dominant culture encourages you to look away from the suffering of others, and even, perhaps, to look away from your own complicity in that suffering. Begin to lean into what emerges for you. If you notice distress, return to your breath and object as anchors. Allow the truth of what your heart is holding to sit with you for a moment and notice how the truth lands in the rest of your body.

You might notice discomfort physically and emotionally, or relief because you are inviting yourself into a practice of being with your heart.

Take a few moments to feel and notice.

As you feel ready, journal about the following:

- How are you feeling after having touched into your heart space?
- What are you holding in your heart at this time?
- How is what you are holding in your heart affecting your mind, body, heart, and spirit?

Once your journaling feels complete, take a moment to read what you've written and reflect. Notice any new emotions that arise.

And now, return to your breath. Take a few deep breaths and repeat the following mantra aloud or silently:

> I feel my heart.
> I acknowledge my heart.
> I feel my heartbeat.
> I acknowledge my heartbeat.

Take a moment to notice how you feel and journal any more thoughts or emotions present at this time.

The spirit is beyond destruction. No one can bring an end to spirit which is everlasting.

—Bhagavad Gita (2:17), *The Living Gita*, commentary by Swami Satchitananda

A LITTLE OF THIS PRACTICE

I was traveling to Honesdale, Pennsylvania, to film a series for Yoga International (YI) that was focused on content from my first book, *Skill in Action: Radicalizing Your Yoga Practice to Create a Just World. Skill in Action* is centered on the intersection of social justice and yoga, inviting readers to make changes in their lives to create a world that allows all of us to be free. Most of my work up until this point has revolved around the content in that book, my years leading Dismantling Racism training, and my time spent as a clinical social worker, yoga teacher, and student. YI invited me to lead an online course for yoga teachers, the bulk of which was influenced by my lived experience as a Black person, activist, and yoga teacher, as well as my book. I had been to Honesdale once before to film a class that was focused on climate change and activism with my friend and colleague Sierra Hollister, and from that experience, I knew Honesdale was a predominantly white town.

Over the course of a few days, YI filmed me as I shared content and curriculum from *Skill in Action*. I shared about the importance of yoga, teachers infusing their teachings with social justice, and engaging yoga philosophy as a tool for creating patterns to counter dominance, supremacy, and oppression. I shared about the breath being central to the practice of yoga, and about how oppression affects our ability to breathe. I reinforced the yogic principle that there is no separation between sentient beings and the planet. We are interconnected and interdependent. Therefore, the ways we suffer, remove the causes of suffering, find freedom, and create conditions for liberation are bound. I was excited to see my work growing, and I was excited about the potential of reaching more people, hopefully inspiring them to create a just world.

I wrapped up filming on the third day and prepared to leave for Philadelphia to teach a weekend workshop in a yoga studio. I packed up my belongings, said goodbye to my Airbnb, and got into my rental car. As I left the Airbnb, less than a block away from it, I saw a police car and I received an intuitive hit that I was going to be stopped and pulled over by the police officer, who stared at me as I drove by.

I have a deep relationship with my intuition and have learned to differentiate my intuition from my anxious thoughts, which are often not based in my deep, inner-knowing. It would have made sense for me, a Black person, to be anxious in a predominantly white town, but the intuitive hit I received was from a place of lived experience and ancestral trauma and wisdom; a place of knowing that Black people have been stopped, harassed, abused, and murdered by the criminal justice system and system of policing for centuries.

Once I realized my intuitive hit felt like a punch, I started to breathe deeply and strategize about what to do if I was pulled over. I slowly drove around the block, while also trying to figure out which direction I needed to go to get out of town. The police car followed me. My GPS kept repeating "Rerouting." I was lost. I went around the block again, put on my turn signal, and quickly made a left-hand turn to head in the right direction.

The police officer followed one more time and then pulled me over in front of the hospital in Honesdale.

I panicked, but somehow had enough clarity to call the only person I really knew in Honesdale—Emily, a staff member at YI. I blurted out what was happening the minute she answered. As I was on the phone with Emily, the police officer came up to my car window and asked if I was lost, to which I replied yes. He asked where I was headed and whether or not I had automobile insurance. I told him it was a rental car, but I knew it was routine for police officers to look up license plates prior to approaching the vehicles of the person they have stopped.

As some small way of letting him know I understood that he stopped me for being Black and was seeking answers that might implicate me just because I am Black, I made a point to tell him he probably already knew it was a rental. I wanted him to understand this wasn't the first time I had been stopped by a white police officer for being Black, and I wanted him to know that I understood how the system and sequence of trying to validate Black people as criminals worked.

He heard Emily on the phone asking me where I was, and he asked who I was talking to. I told him, and he then went on to ask why I called someone. "I feel safer with her knowing where I am," I responded. The officer then asked for my license, which I handed to him, and he asked for the car's registration, which I knew might be in the glove compartment. I reacted by saying, "I am not going to reach into the glove compartment. You can reach in there, but I will not."

This isn't the first time I have stopped myself from reaching for the glove compartment after having been pulled over. As a Black woman, I know it isn't safe to move or to reach into compartments in a car when you are stopped by the police. This automatic reaction of knowing when and how to move is deeply embedded into my being. I have watched too many videos of police stops where a Black person has slowly reached into the glove compartment, or had their hands up, or waved their hands outside of their car immediately after being pulled over, or they've promptly disclosed they have a registered weapon, and the scenario resulted in them ending up dead. As he was staring at my North Carolina license, he replied, "I don't know where you're from or how it is where you're from . . . "

I can't remember how he completed that sentence. My mind was distracted by the memory of Sandra Bland, who was stopped for a minor traffic violation, and I was thinking about how that experience led to her death. I was thinking about my mother and how she didn't know where I was, and I was thinking of my partner and how far away he was.

Without my asking, Emily asked, "Where are you? I'll be right there." I didn't exactly know where I was and described the buildings around me, the hospital next to me, and the parking deck next to it. When Emily arrived, she stood on the sidewalk between my car and the police car. She asked if I was okay.

I don't remember how I answered that question. I wasn't okay. Nothing about the situation was okay. I was afraid. I was trying to keep my cool, manage my trauma, and strategize how to keep myself safe and alive. I knew Emily's presence might escalate the situation, and I also knew that in this situation, her whiteness might be the thing that could keep me safe. She was concerned and upset, and she asked the police officer why I had been pulled over.

Emily—a white woman—came to support me—a Black woman—which most certainly was a threat to the officer and system of white supremacy. She told the officer he stopped me for driving while Black, which felt true to me, but wasn't something I would ever say; in my experience, when Blackness challenges white power, the consequences can be grave.

The officer did not like Emily questioning him, and at some point, he came back to my car to tell me how dangerous it can be to have someone interfere with a police stop. He gave me directions to the next town and sent me on my way. I left without a ticket and with no honest explanation of why I was pulled over.

Once Emily and I left the scene in our separate cars, we pulled over to the building where the *Skill in Action* course had been filmed. I was shaken to my core. As we got out of our cars, I was crying, and I found it challenging to breathe. I had just spent three days talking about the breath as a metaphor for liberation. I had spoken about how oppression takes the breath away. And here I was, unable to find my own breath in the immediate aftermath of being stopped by a police officer. Emily and I walked next to a stream as I tried to regulate my breathing and nervous system, both of which had gone haywire.

I shared with Emily about how much pain I felt. It wasn't physical pain; it was more emotional and spiritual. Once again, I realized how important my work to create conditions for justice is, and how risky it is to be doing this work in a Black body. The work I do is soul work—it doesn't feel like a choice for me; it feels like a calling that I have to continually answer. What struck me the most about the police officer stopping me that time was that I was doing my soul's work, which is about dismantling white supremacy and systems of oppression. And as I was doing this work, I was reminded that my life could be taken in a moment by a white police officer and by a racist criminal justice system in a white supremacist culture. Both of these awarenesses generated dissonance in my body and spirit.

I followed Emily to the next town and then she drove back to Honesdale while I continued my drive to Philadelphia. I felt shell-shocked the whole drive. Prior to being stopped by the police officer, I had known full well that the world wasn't safe; my lack of safety felt even more acute after being pulled over.

I made it to Philadelphia, checked into my Airbnb, and went to find some food to nourish myself as a way of regulating my nervous system. I had the same feeling I always have after a traumatic experience—it's the feeling that everyone can see something is wrong. And in the restaurant where I went to get dinner, I found myself imagining what it might be like if people saw the words "I just got stopped for driving while Black" tattooed on my forehead. I imagined what it might be like to tell someone in the restaurant what happened and for us to have a conversation about racial profiling. The absence of someone there supporting me in real time, as Emily had, made me long for someone to see my fragility and vulnerability.

The next morning, I prepared to teach a *Skill in Action* workshop. I hadn't planned to tell the class about what happened, and yet I told them within the first thirty minutes. I was almost in tears as I let them know I had been pulled over by a police officer, that I was feeling tender and traumatized, and that I wasn't going to be my best self during our time together. I made it through the weekend teaching about anti-racism, justice, and yoga, and then I returned home to North Carolina.

The week after the police stop was hazy. I remember feeling sad, then depressed, and then angry—all of which are signs of grief. I didn't have energy, and I felt very unmotivated as I prepared for more travel and three more *Skill in Action* workshops. I flew to Portland to work for a few days and started to feel sick. I blamed it on the man sniffling behind me on the plane en route to Portland. I went from Portland to Los Angeles and became congested, had a sore throat, and I felt increasingly and completely depleted. I stayed in bed for an entire day while taking copious amounts of wellness formula, drinking more orange juice then I usually drink throughout a year, taking honey, elderberry syrup, Throat Coat tea, and eventually, taking Sudafed. I blamed this sudden illness on travel and planes, but in hindsight, my body was trying to rid itself of the residual trauma of being stopped by the police officer the prior week.

Grief shows up in many ways. For me, grief manifests most strongly physically, and then emotionally. It's as if my body has to completely shut down for me to recognize that I need to make space to grieve. While I lay there sick in Los Angeles, my body was working hard to slow me down and to clear the trauma arising from living in a culture that creates conditions that put me at risk because of my racial identity. This type of trauma comes from fearing for my life because of the number of Black and Brown people whose lives have been taken at the hands of police and other institutions designed to create unjust conditions for Black, Indigenous, and People of Color (BIPOC). I grieved with an awareness that my experience wasn't unique. People who are marginalized by unjust institutions and systems feel anger, sadness, confusion, and depression. Marginalization causes dis-ease physically, mentally, emotionally, and spiritually because of the weight of holding grief while responding to systems that continue to cause grief.

Collective grief is what is experienced by communities when their sense of safety is challenged or stripped away. So many of us have had our sense of safety compromised by trauma, war, planetary devastation, natural disasters, and pandemics. The collective grief that arises from marginalization and injustice originates from the experience of continual confrontations with oppression, like being silenced, policed, and made invisible; cultural appropriation and erasure; and the legacy of enslavement of Black bodies and colonization.

When I don't make space to grieve, the grief doesn't vanish or disappear; it gets held in my body, heart, spirit, and mind. It can result in sadness, anger, depression, anxiety, physical ailments, and heartbreak, which tends to increase or amplify until I either engage maladaptive coping strategies to deny my grief, or strategies to heal by turning toward it and allowing myself to process and recover. My body and spirit needed time to grieve and recover from the encounter with the Honesdale police officer. Instead, I had committed to teaching several workshops in Portland and Los Angeles, and I chose to follow through on the commitment I had made. Teaching and holding space were difficult at that time. But, my teaching and spiritual practice, particularly inspired by the story of the Bhagavad Gita, became part of the medicine I needed to grieve, recover, and heal.

The Bhagavad Gita is an ancient text that has profoundly influenced me. *Bhagavad Gita* means "the song of the Blessed One." It begins with the warrior, Arjuna, being driven in a chariot to the open space between two armies. Krishna is the chariot driver and he is Arjuna's guide. Arjuna is instructed to fight in the war, yet when he goes out on the battlefield, he encounters people he knows on both sides of the fight and he throws down his weapons. He shares with Krishna that he doesn't want to fight, and that the other warriors should kill him. Krishna responds to Arjuna by telling him that souls cannot die because souls aren't born. He says to Arjuna, "Bodies die, but the essence of who you are, Arjuna, is everlasting." (2.18) Krishna is teaching Arjuna to broaden his perspective beyond the moment so he can realize that his soul is bigger than his physical body. In realizing this, he can follow through on what he is being tasked with: fighting a war.

Throughout the Bhagavad Gita, Krishna teaches Arjuna ways to support him in remembering his soul's everlasting nature. With Krishna's guidance, Arjuna learns philosophy, lessons, rituals, and practices that prepare him to live into his dharma or duty. Likewise, the Bhagavad Gita offers us many lessons. It instructs us about how to respond to the internal war so many of us are battling due to cultural conditioning, family background, ancestral wounds, trauma, and all the ways the mind spins us into mental traps that make it difficult to remember our true nature and divinity. The Bhagavad Gita also teaches us to detach from results and engage in our dharma—to live into our higher purpose, regardless of whether we see the fruits of our labor. The ancient text teaches that change is the law of the universe, and the text offers different ways to engage spiritual practice, be it the path of knowledge, action, or devotion.

As I taught my workshops that weekend, lessons from the Bhagavad Gita helped me begin to process my grief and remember my dharma. Two quotes kept appearing in my consciousness as I led my workshop participants in a practice of actionable yoga.

Never was there a time when I did not exist, or you, or
these kings; nor will there come a time when we
cease to be. (2.12)
No effort is wasted, no gain ever reversed; even a little of
this practice will shelter you from sorrow. (2.40)
—The Bhagavad Gita

The first verse reminded me that there will not be a time when the essence of who I am will cease to be. Remembering this affirmed that I am a soul and spirit much bigger than the confines of my human body, and that I have a responsibility to live into my dharma and purpose in this lifetime. The second verse reminded me of the medicinal healing qualities of spiritual practice. The practice of yoga creates a path to both engage in the work of acknowledging the importance of our efforts and to simultaneously move through the grief, sorrow, heaviness, and despair that surface as we respond to our internal and external wars. The wisdom the Bhagavad Gita offered me throughout the weekend and beyond is what prompted me to make space to grieve and process with the awareness that I have a practice to hold me through it all.

My body took its time to recover from the experience I had in Honesdale. To some extent, I am still processing, recovering, and digesting that incident and all my other lived experiences of oppression. When I got home from that trip, my spiritual practice helped me to rest, go inward, and ask myself what needed my attention. My practice included meditation, prayer, yoga nidra, divination tools, movement, and chanting mantras to shift the vibration in my heart. Once again, my practice became a safe harbor and supported me in staying grounded amid the internal dysregulation I was experiencing alongside the external dysregulation—the chaos of the world—that was affecting me. My practice didn't always lift the sadness or rage I felt, but it did allow me to feel emotions and it helped me invite them to flow through me, knowing that they would shift. As the Bhagavad Gita teaches, change is the law of the universe.

Although occasionally I don't know I'm grieving until I'm sick in bed or until I slow down enough to feel what is present before me, I am thankful for the ability to grieve. I am thankful for the container that spiritual practice creates for my grief. Your individual and our collective grief deserve to be seen, held, felt, and cared for. Spiritual practice can hold it all.

A spiritual practice, whether it be movement, meditation, prayer, withdrawing the senses to go inward, or remembering our connection with Spirit, is a gift one can return to time and time again. A practice rooted in bringing one back to the truth of who they are can be grounding amid the process of encountering grief and the vast journey that grieving entails. Spiritual practice is the well we can revisit to support us as we grieve and attempt to mend our hearts. As we turn to our spiritual practices to help heal and support us, we must also remember spiritual practice is about awakening and becoming aware—it is not about bypassing our collective trauma. Spiritual practice provides a tool that is meant to assist us in leaning into all that is causing us to grieve, illuminating that which is true and real.

PRACTICE
Sadhana

For this practice, you will need your journal and a pen or pencil. You will cultivate a practice you can engage in for forty days.

In spiritual spaces, often this is called a sadhana, which means "dedicated practice." We will begin with a centering to help you prepare to journal about your sadhana.

We will start with a breathing practice to quiet your mind.

Find a comfortable seat, or if you prefer, you can stand or lie down. You might want to elevate your hips by sitting on a cushion, pillow, or blanket.

Close your eyes or soften your gaze to the ground in front of you, and begin to breathe into your body. Start by taking deep breaths in and out. Begin to feel the shape change in your body as you breathe in and out. Notice the expansion as you breathe in and the contraction or release with each exhale.

Now, continue to breathe and begin to match the length of your inhale and exhale. This equal-part breathing can help offer clarity and quiet the mind.

Sit for at least three minutes practicing equal-part breathing. Notice the physical sensations and the emotions that arise.

As you are ready, begin to move out of your meditation and take a moment to consider a practice you would like to commit to for forty days as a way of acknowledging and responding to whatever you might be grieving at this time. I suggest a practice that is five to ten minutes to begin, with awareness that you can increase the time you practice as you move through the sadhana.

You might think about different types of meditation—sitting, walking, standing, or lying down. You might decide your sadhana will be a movement practice of the same postures for a set amount of time, each day for forty days. Perhaps you want to practice pranayama. You could practice yoga nidra. Maybe you want to chant or work with a mantra, repeating it to yourself during a meditation each morning or as you work with a mala. Think of a practice, but do not think too much—the mind tends to step in, making us interrupt our creative flow and imagination.

Once you have settled on a practice, journal about the following:

- What specific practice have you chosen for your sadhana?
- What resources might you need to support you in fully engaging in your sadhana?
- What will you remind yourself of if you begin to feel unmotivated to practice?
- What gentle statement can you say to yourself if you skip a day of your practice?

After you have finished journaling, write down this statement: *I commit to practice (insert practice) for forty days.* Now repeat the statement three times aloud.

Begin your practice either the day you move through this *Finding Refuge* activity or the following day. A note about sadhanas: If you miss a day of practice, you begin again the next day, starting a new forty-day cycle. If you miss a day, please do not be hard on yourself; be kind and gentle—most of us forget to practice at times. The practice *is* a way to find refuge, and you might discover a practice you would like to engage in well beyond the initial forty days. If it would feel supportive to journal about your experience of your sadhana as you move through it, please do so.

There is something in the depths of our being that hungers for wholeness.

—Thomas Merton,
No Man Is an Island

WHOLENESS

It was June 30, 2017, when I started my trek across the country from Carrboro, North Carolina, to Portland, Oregon. I was moving to start a job with an organization and a group of people I was very excited to work with and learn from. On the day of my departure from Carrboro, I went on a canoe ride that felt like a final voyage, as if my life wouldn't be the same once I boarded the plane with my sweet pup, Jasper. A great blue heron led my partner, Charles, and me on the canoe ride, flying from tree limb to sandy island to tall branches in a cluster of trees. Heron animal medicine is a medicine I have carried for quite some time. It is connected to following one's path, grounding yourself by connecting to the earth, and learning how to become comfortable with uncertainty. The heron led us to a magical place where we saw dozens of herons—mamas, grandmas, papas, babies, whole families of herons. A feather fell from the sky, landing in the water, and I wanted to grab it to take with me as a symbol of my last day in North Carolina, and to recognize my first day of a new journey.

I carried the heron feather with me on the airplane, flying first-class while Jasper ate popcorn at my feet. When we arrived, I waited in baggage claim for the mighty amount of luggage I had checked onto the plane. I boarded the bus for the rental car center and a woman, who saw me with my overflowing luggage cart and dog in tow, said, "You're going to make it. You're going to be alright." I look back at that moment and think she was a wise sage, foretelling the future of what was to come over the next year. I felt a mixture of excitement, sadness, and adventure, and I longed for an anchor: home.

The Monday after I arrived in Portland, I began my new job. I was greeted with a sweet care package in my office from the staff. The care package included a journal, a picture frame with a photo of Mt. Willing Road in North Carolina, and some chocolate. Mt. Willing Road was a road I always passed on my way to hair appointments. It struck me the first time I passed by it because I thought about what it takes to be willing to climb a mountain—determination, strength, the awareness of when it is time to rest and perseverance.

It was almost as if my new colleagues knew the challenges and lessons to come would stem directly from whether or not we had the capacity to show one another care and prioritize wholeness as individuals and as a collective group working toward a common goal. I was a seasoned facilitator with two decades of work behind me, and I felt confident in my ability to lead in this new work setting. I believed in our work as anti-racism trainers and our mission and vision for the world. I believed it was possible to cultivate healing from personal, institutional, and cultural oppression—within ourselves, our own organization, and in the organizations we partnered with.

After my first week in Portland, I had made a few friends, started to acclimate to my new job, and was settling into my new home, which had the most magical fireplace I have ever seen, adorned with red jasper, amethyst, quartz, and many other healing crystals. Over the next year, that fireplace would become a monument, representing all the losses I would endure, and it would become a magical portal, holding the stories of all the women who gathered in my home for full-moon circles to release what no longer served them. At the time of my move from North Carolina to Portland, I had no idea how massive the losses and connections I had to release would be. I moved away from North Carolina to release part of who I was and to get closer to the truth of who I wanted to be.

The lessons from the heron began shortly after I arrived when a very unexpected loss occurred in my life: my father died eleven days after I moved to Portland. When I heard the news, I was out, walking Jasper and considering the list of ingredients I needed to prepare dinner for a new friend I had just invited to my home. I was walking down Madison Street and rounding the corner onto 44th when I received a phone call. It was my mother. I could immediately tell that something was wrong. She nervously blurted out, "I have something to tell you." I thought she was going to tell me my grandmother had passed away. Instead, she said, "Your father passed away."

After my mother told me the news, I remember stopping in my tracks. It became very difficult to breathe. I knew I had to make it back to my house quickly—I was about to fall apart, unsure of how to process the message my mother had just shared with me. I called my best friend, Amy, who was in Portland en route to Seattle, her home, and she turned around to come be with me. I called my other friend, also named Amy, who was joining me for dinner, and through my tears, I invited her to decide whether or not she wanted to come witness me in the disheveled and disembodied state I was in. Both came over with dinner in hand, and we sat outside and built a fire in the chiminea while Jasper kept barking at the trees, which convinced all of us my father's spirit was present.

My father's energy and spirit felt very unsettled. We asked for him to have an easy transition. The truth is, nothing was easy about this situation. We burned bundles of sage, drank wine, and I kept feeling the shockwave of moving to a new place, barely having landed, and then suffering the loss of a parent with whom I'd had a very complicated relationship.

A year before I moved to Portland, I had a dream about my father dying. In the dream, I came home to Jeff, my ex-husband, who was cutting up vegetables in the kitchen. When I walked into the kitchen, he blurted out, "Your father has died. Listen to the message on the answering machine." I replied, "I know." I went into the living room to listen to the message and all I heard was garble, as if my father couldn't really communicate. It sounded like he was underwater, just like my mother had been when she was close to death and speaking with the ancestors. In my father's voicemail, I could tell he was sick and wanted to share something with me, but I couldn't decipher his message. This dream about his death was in my consciousness until the day he died.

I hadn't seen my father in seven years. Since our last visit, I had spoken to him on occasion, but had not seen him in the flesh. The last time I did see him he was in Tucson, Arizona, a few hours away from his home in Prescott. He was in the veteran's hospital in a program that was designed to support veterans who were going blind. To be honest, I had forgotten my father was a veteran and that he had been in the navy. He was only there for a short stint and I was told he was discharged because of his asthma. My father, mother, and I were all fated with bronchial asthma.

My father, Cornelius Johnson, once a pro football player, now had diabetes, heart disease, was going blind, and was a double amputee. My stepmother dropped him off at the hospital without any money, clothing, or items to meet his basic needs during his stay. Jeff and I had visited my father every day, giving him money, making sure he had enough food to eat, and buying him underwear, T-shirts, chewing gum, and other sundries. We once took him out to eat, and I watched as he sat at the table and burst into tears. We immediately drove him back to the hospital. He settled down a bit, but much like the message I couldn't decipher on the answering machine in my dream, I couldn't decipher what was causing him so much distress; he found it difficult to communicate through his tears. We encouraged him to rest and went back to visit him the following day.

When we arrived, my father was exhibiting the symptoms I had seen in the clients I worked with in my clinical social work practice: he was emotionally dysregulated, anxious, and afraid. He was exhibiting signs of PTSD, and I knew I was preparing for what would become one of the most poignant moments in my social work career.

My father disclosed the real story of why he left the navy. He told me of a navy ship captain who had sexually assaulted him, not once but multiple times. As my father disclosed this story and recounted his trauma to me, I did what I tend to do in crisis situations—I went into full-on social work mode, and I let the part of me that was his daughter sit back while I made plans for him to get a psychological consult and begin therapy.

What came in my reflection much later was that my father's story of trauma explained some of his erratic, controlling, and dissociative behavior. My father was a Black man in the navy in the late-1960s. At that time, sexual violence against men wasn't something that was discussed or believed to happen, especially not male-on-male sexual violence. After my father was sexually assaulted, he became a pro football player and described becoming a machine on the field. Robotic, tough, and invincible. He became hypermasculine to try to heal wounds that were invisible to others. As he sat in the VA hospital sharing his truth with me, his wounds were being exposed and he was tender. I was too.

After my father died, I spent the next several days trying to keep myself busy while feeling completely ungrounded. The shockwave of his death continued to reverberate and I didn't have the emotional reserves to reground myself—I had used all my reserves in uprooting my life and moving across the country, not expecting a personal crisis right after I landed.

Prior to my move to Portland, my mother had sent money for me to purchase a dining room table. She knew how much I loved to entertain, and the fact that tables—especially when they are in the warmth of kitchens, meant to nurture—represent home to me. I was in a grief haze when I entered IKEA in search of the perfect dining table the very day after my father passed away. I remember trying to remove a shopping cart from the exit instead of the entrance. My mind was hazy and my heart fractured; I didn't understand the IKEA cart system, nor did I observe the large red exit sign above the line of shopping carts. I struggled with the carts, trying to force one to release from the others, as two women gazed at me as if I was not in my right mind. Grief will make one do things that don't make sense to other people.

After a while, I freed the shopping cart and spent two hours wandering the aisles of IKEA, finally finding what would become my dining room table. All I had to do was assemble it. I knew it would be a challenge to put it together—I had a knack for putting things together backward and then having to undo them and put them together again. I sat on the floor with bolts and random parts, trying to figure out how they would fit. My own self felt like the various parts on the floor—I wasn't sure how my pieces fit, and I wasn't sure how I was going to put myself back together. It took hours, but I finally got the table assembled.

I remember grocery shopping after my father passed away—I moved at a snail's pace through the aisles, wanting to scream at the top of my lungs, "My father died! What does one do when their father dies?" And "Why can't you see I'm suffering!" I wanted everyone to see the suffering I was experiencing as an extension of their own suffering because we are truly connected in this way. I longed for these random folks in the Fred Meyer grocery store to turn toward me and to extend care. I imagine this was a similar feeling to how my father felt, having to hold the secret of his assault inside for so long. If he made space for his own suffering and grief, he did so silently and in isolation.

After a few days, I went back to work. My colleagues hugged me and tried to tend to my emotional state, which was something bigger than sadness. I attempted to work, but I truly didn't give a shit. At work, the pace sped up, and all I wanted to do was slow down. We led anti-racism trainings to transform behavior and culture, while our own work culture continued to be so steeped in white supremacy. Money was prioritized over people, we had unreasonable deadlines, and workaholism was seen as a strength and asset in the organization. We had no business trying to train anyone on transformation. But the saying is true: "We teach what we need." I stood in front of rooms defining white supremacy and racism, holding space by inviting people into embodiment, while feeling like a fraud: I was working in an institution that allowed productivity and business goals to overpower our ability to prioritize wholeness, healing, and centering our trauma and grief in response to individual losses and the losses our work was meant to respond to—white supremacy and systems of oppression.

This experience wasn't new to me; it was a pattern that had repeated often, much like a broken record that skips, unable to complete the beauty of its song or sound. This pattern was so familiar to me because it had been institutionalized as normal in so many organizations I had worked for and with—workplaces inhabited by good people who weren't given the space to process how the work was affecting them, or the space to slow down long enough to center the gravity of what it means to try to heal highly adaptable systems of oppression focused on fragmentation and divide and conquer. When we don't prioritize wholeness, oppression wins.

Social movements begin when people say, "No more of this; we are tired and fed up, and we must take action." Collectives form to interrupt, disrupt, intervene, grieve, and build new ways of being that are counter to the toxicity of dominant culture. Social movements and collectives die because we replicate systems of oppression when we don't engage in spiritual practice, radical and collective care, or grieve the tragedies our movements respond to. Collectives die when we don't prioritize healing, integrity, and wholeness as much as we prioritize the work. Many nonprofits and social change spaces are in the business of addressing what is so desperately flawed in our culture, while at the same time replicating the patterns they are trying to disrupt. This can show up as workaholism, a lack of empathy, a practice of protecting dysfunctional behavior at the expense of everyone in an organization, power hoarding, perfectionism, a lack of self and collective care, little to no time for staff to connect, and valuing productivity over centering relationship with staff and community.

Each of these behaviors is deeply rooted in white supremacy culture and representative of how white supremacy can look in action. I learned about the patterns of white supremacy from my friend and colleague Tema Okun. She and my former colleague, Kenneth Jones, wrote an article titled, "White Supremacy Culture," to support organizations in identifying how white supremacy shows up. The article also offers information about antidotes to the toxicity that white supremacy breeds.*

Culture is created through norms, values, beliefs, standards, and expectations. Dominant culture assumes one group is superior and another inferior based on identities it has deemed as "normal" and "abnormal." Dominant culture is based on a system of dominance and superiority, enacted through policy and practice in institutions and through cultural norms, standards, values, beliefs, and expectations. Systems such as racism, sexism, heterosexism, ableism, ageism, and many others are interlocked, working together to create or restrict opportunities. These systems enable some people to live with closer proximity to power, while others are deemed as undeserving and undesirable, and kept further away from power and from the ability to be well and

* Tema Okun, "White Supremacy Culture," Dismantling Racism (website), https://www.dismantlingracism.org/uploads/4/3/5/7/43579015/okun_-_white _sup_culture.pdf.

whole. Dominant culture values being white, heterosexual, male, able-bodied, and young as identities worthy of survival. It devalues being a person of color, LGBTQ, female, disabled, and/or an elder as identities undeserving of the ability to thrive.

CULTURAL TRAUMA

Many of us think of trauma as an individual, isolated experience, similar to my mother's experience of physical and emotional trauma from her illness and her fight to survive, or my father's traumatic experience of being sexually assaulted. But my mother's illness was neither isolated nor individual. She is not the first Black woman who has received substandard care from a medical institution.

There is a long history of medical institutions and the system of health care offering subpar services to Black women, and there is a long history of denial of care to Black people; dominant culture perpetuates the belief that Black women and Black people don't deserve the same level of care (or sometimes, any care at all) as white people. My father's experience of being sexually assaulted by a white superior in the navy wasn't isolated or individual. He isn't the first Black man who white supremacy has tried to control by any means necessary. There is a history of physical and sexual violence being used as a form of oppression that dates back to the days of my ancestors being enslaved by white slave owners.

The perpetuation of the norms that Black people don't deserve care and that Black people must be physically, emotionally, mentally, psychically, and spiritually controlled, and the actions emerging from these cultural norms, are representative of the many ways that dominant culture produces harm and trauma.

When a group of people experiences life-threatening trends because dominant culture deems one or more identities they embody as unworthy, the individual experience of trauma expands and becomes a collective experience or cultural trauma.

The legal scholar Angela Onwuachi-Willig defines cultural traumas as "socially mediated processes that occur when groups endure horrific events that forever change their consciousness and identity. According to cultural sociologists, these traumas arise out of shocks to the routine or the taken for granted. Understanding such traumas is critical for developing solutions that can address group suffering."* Dominant culture conditions us not to see or name the harm and cultural trauma it produces, such as war, genocide, terrorism, and natural disasters caused by human manipulations of our environment. Those who embody multiple marginalized identities are more likely to experience individual and cultural trauma at a higher rate than those with closer proximity to power and the identities that enact dominance. In the United States, Black men, Black trans women, and Latinx and Muslim immigrants, for example, experience physical violence and cultural trauma at high rates due to the negative cultural norms about these groups of people at this time. It has become normal to traumatize whole communities by denying their ability to move through life with ease and a sense of belonging.

Dominant culture asks us to normalize the harm it creates as it marginalizes people instead of framing what is happening as traumatic. Dominant culture asks us to deny oppression is

* Angela Onwuachi-Willig, "The Trauma of the Routine: Lessons on Cultural Trauma from the Emmett Till Verdict," *Sociological Theory* 34, no. 4 (December 2016), https://scholarship.law.bu.edu/faculty_scholarship/294/.

happening, forget our history and the lasting impacts of colonialism, and pretend we are not implicated in systems of marginalization, which only advances the suffering of the collective whole. When the heartbreak that comes from being alive at this time is normalized or numbed, it creates a sense of helplessness, hopelessness, apathy, and fatigue so deep that it resides in the bones, cells, and tissues. When our trauma goes unattended and unresolved, I believe we risk the death of some part of ourselves, if not the whole of who we are.

Scale this to the collective. As a collective, we are heartbroken and heartsick; we are allowing grief to take up residence in our bones, cells, and tissues without processing it. If you are experiencing hypervigilance, fear, anxiety, depression, grief, PTSD, hopelessness, or helplessness in response to dominant culture, you are experiencing cultural trauma.

My desire to make this spinning planet pause to notice our collective experience of cultural trauma isn't new. I often feel a hankering to scream, "We are dying! We are dying, and we are killing one another. We are sick, and we aren't interested in being well. We are entitled, and our entitlement is causing oppression and suffering. We must stop. If we do not, we will not survive." This is how I feel about what has occurred and what continues to occur during unsettling and uncertain times in our country and the world. I want everything to pause. I want us to pause long enough to notice the patterns of harm and the systems of oppression that continue to multiply, and I want us to pause long enough to recognize our responsibility to interrupt them. I want us to pause long enough to make space for our grief.

If we allow overwhelm and trauma to consume us, then we won't be able to grieve or heal. If we do not begin to recognize the air we are breathing in as toxic and the water we are swimming in as dangerous, we will not heal. Our job is to understand what culture is made of and where we are implicated in perpetuating cultural trauma, as well as how we are experiencing it so that we can shift our own behavior, resist overwhelm, and make an offering to heal the collective.

The only viable response to cultural trauma is healing individually and in community, even as we feel brokenhearted about the cultural conditions that deprioritize our wholeness and humanity. Spiritual practice reminds us that it is possible to remember our wholeness even as dominant culture tries to split us apart individually and collectively.

PRACTICE
Moving into Wholeness

For this practice, you will need your journal and the object that you have chosen to use for the *Finding Refuge* process.

We will start with a breathing practice to quiet your mind.

Find a comfortable seat, or if you prefer, you can stand or lie down. Place your object next to you or near you. You might want to elevate your hips by sitting on a cushion, pillow, or blanket.

Close your eyes or soften your gaze to the ground in front of you, and begin to breathe into your body. Start by taking deep breaths in and out. Begin to feel the shape change in your body as you breathe in and out. Notice the expansion as you breathe in, and the contraction or release with your exhale. Begin to notice the upward energy as you inhale and the downward energy as you exhale.

Breathe deeply into your body, noticing the physical sensations and emotions. Notice any spaces of tension or resistance, and respond to them with a deeper breath.

Bring your awareness to an image in your mind's eye that represents integrity, wholeness, and healing for you. This can be a landscape, a person or being, or any other image that represents integrity, wholeness, and healing. Notice everything you can about this image.

Now bring your awareness to your whole self, the whole of your experience in this moment. Consider how dominant culture conditions us not to be whole or in alignment; this moment is an invitation for you to fully be yourself. Breathe, and if possible, connect with an embodied sense of joy. Breathe, and if possible, connect with the parts of yourself that are yet to be fully understood.

Please take a moment to journal, draw, or collage your image.

With a connection to your image of integrity, wholeness, and healing as well as your own wholeness, repeat the following mantra:

> I am whole.
> I am healing.
> We are whole.
> We are healing.

Repeat this mantra as many times as you would like. Notice what arises as the mantra soaks into your awareness and experience.

Once you feel ready to move out of meditation, with each breath cycle, bring your awareness back to the expansion and the contraction/release, as well as the energy flow in your body.

Know you can carry the mantra with you throughout your day. I encourage you to come back to the mantra as you interact with others, seeing their wholeness and humanity.

If possible, hold or connect with your object that represents wholeness as a reminder that, as you do the work of deepening your awareness of how dominant culture has asked you to be a fragment of who you truly are, you are whole as you are.

Lastly, take a moment to reflect on the following question: *What will support you in remembering your wholeness?*

Grief is praise, because it is the natural way love honors what it misses.

—Martin Prechtel,
*The Smell of Rain on Dust:
Grief and Praise*

ENLARGED HEARTS

It was a few days after the Christmas holiday and my mother and grandmother had come to North Carolina for a visit. They had chosen to stay in Richmond for Christmas but decided to come visit us right after the holiday to continue to celebrate. At the time, our house was being completely renovated. Jeff and I were living in my in-laws' rental house with our sweet dog, Maggie. The back half of the house was being redone with a new kitchen, pottery studio, two bathrooms, and an upstairs bedroom. The house was being gutted from the inside out. Little did we know that our lives were about to be gutted as well by the news of the loss of a dear friend.

The first evening my mother and grandmother were there, I had decided to make dinner and debunk my mother's narrative about my lack of cooking skills. I made chicken parmesan and a salad, and everyone seemed to enjoy the meal. The following afternoon, Jeff and I were preparing to go to a wedding ceremony for a friend and former colleague. I was sitting on the couch putting on my high heels, almost ready to leave, and I decided to check my email. I saw an email from my friend, Laura, the wife of my close friend, Eric Diener.

The subject line in the email from Laura read, "About Eric." I opened it, and read it over in disbelief. Laura's email said that they had been out to dinner in Wetumpka, Alabama, and were paying their bill as they prepared to leave the restaurant. Laura heard Eric try to say something to her, but when she turned toward him, he fell on the back of his chair and knocked over an empty chair behind him. He had what appeared to be a seizure and was unconscious. After being taken to the ER and unconscious for fifty minutes, the doctors were able to resuscitate Eric. He was transferred to a hospital in Montgomery, and he was there when I received the email from Laura. He was in the ICU, unable to breathe on his own. His heart muscles were very weak, and it was likely that he had a cardiac arrest and a blood clot that traveled from his heart to his brain. The CT scan of his lungs showed mild pneumonia, and his heart and brain had been without oxygen for a long time—the damage to these organs was significant. She believed it would take another couple days before they would know more about the prognosis of his condition.

I was in shock and disbelief upon reading this email. I couldn't believe it was referencing my thirty-nine-year-old friend. I shared the news with Jeff, and we felt the impulse to go be with Eric, but we had a wedding to attend. I called Laura and she told us to wait until the next day to come and see them. She told me that she thought Eric understood what was happening, and that at times, he had tears streaming down his face. He couldn't talk, but Laura felt like he knew the gravity of his condition.

Jeff and I went to our friend's wedding and tried to be in a celebratory mood, but our minds and hearts were with Eric and his family. The next morning, I received a phone call from Laura: Eric had passed away earlier that day. As Laura shared the news with me, I heard her words, but couldn't process them. I was in shock. I went into the guest room to tell my mom and grandmother the news and I burst into tears. Without my saying anything, my mother knew that Eric was gone. We sat on the edge of the bed and my mother held me as I sobbed.

During the days after Eric's passing, I communicated the news with friends, wrote his obituary for our local paper, spoke with his parents, and supported Laura in planning a gathering at their home in Asheville, North Carolina. I handled the details and automatically went into planning mode, not as a way of avoiding my grief—well, at least not consciously—but as a way to honor a friend and beloved who had played such an enormous role in my life. The immensity of Eric's influence on my life matched the deep grief I felt over losing him.

I met Eric in 1996 when I moved to Chapel Hill, North Carolina, to attend UNC–Chapel Hill's School of Social Work. I was classmates with one of his roommates, Tricia, and met him shortly after the first semester began. The first semester of graduate school was challenging: a month after I began school, I was sexually assaulted. After the assault, I went to the hospital and then to Tricia's house. Over the next few days, I slept and cried a lot, communicated with my professors about not being able to come to class, and I avoided going back to my apartment. The assault didn't occur there, but I didn't want to explain to my roommates what had happened and where I had been all weekend. Eric kept his distance, but he was concerned about me. That was the beginning of my relationship with Eric.

He was going through his own trauma at the time; he was separated and getting a divorce. Both of us felt tender and a bit broken; this may have been why the gravitational pull between us was so strong. That first semester, and for a few years to come, Eric became my lover, confidant, and mirror.

When our romantic relationship ended a couple of times, we managed to create a different kind of relationship—a deep and everlasting friendship. I would call Eric for advice and support when I needed it. We would frequently check in with each other, sharing about how our lives were shifting and changing based on new jobs, moves to different towns, homes, pets, or ventures we had begun. As the years went on, Eric became friends with Jeff, and I became friends with Laura. We would all go on long hikes together, and time and time again, Eric would act as if we were lost and then somehow lead us to a beautiful vista looking down into a valley to watch the sunset over the Blue Ridge mountains. This was the essence of Eric: a beautiful vista looking down into a valley in the middle of a mountain range that felt massive, reminding Eric he was a small part of a tremendous and nuanced ecosystem.

An enlarged heart sent a clot to Eric's brain, which caused swelling and ultimately, his death. The doctors weren't sure if his heart was enlarged prior to the blood clot developing or if it came from the impact of trying to resuscitate him. There was one story of him having what seemed like a heart attack in college, but the ER doctors chalked it up to him potentially drinking too much. We all asked questions about his heart, trying to figure out the origin and an explanation for something that truly was unexplainable—our thirty-nine-year-old beloved passing away. Enlarged hearts are believed to come from an underlying issue causing the heart to work harder. I cannot help but think that Eric's enlarged heart came from his sensitivity to the trauma he witnessed and was aware of in his own life and beyond, in the greater world.

One of his responses to the trauma he had experienced and become aware of in the culture was to be of service to others. Eric spent most of his adult life seeking ways to heal the planet and the sentient beings who inhabit her. He worked with an outdoor program teaching youth to hike and overcome their fears by learning survival skills. Much later, he became a guardian ad litem, playing the role of advocate for children who were at risk for being taken away from their families by the Department of Social Services. Eric worked at the Emerson Waldorf School in Chapel Hill, North Carolina, as the business manager, with a mission to make the school more affordable for families of color. He spent time working for the Community Home Trust in Orange County, North Carolina, increasing affordable housing in the county. Eric strove to improve the homes that were built to better serve homebuyers, and he worked hard to ensure that the homes were well-built and affordable.

When Eric passed away, he was working as a green home builder in Asheville because he cared deeply about the environment and understood that we humans were not living in sustainable ways. Even after he died, his big-heartedness and generosity continued as those who loved him and wanted to pay tribute to his life honored his request to support Save the Children. He specifically chose countries that were in critical need of support: Zimbabwe, the Congo, the Gaza Strip, Pakistan, and Afghanistan.

Eric's heart felt deeply. I was not surprised to hear it was enlarged. It made perfect sense to me—I knew his heart, and I am forever grateful for having had the opportunity to be in his life in this physical world, and to continue a connection with him in the spirit world.

• • •

At this time on our planet, many of us are feeling sensitive to the trauma that is happening to and around us. We are responding to things we have never experienced before—a pandemic, disconnection from others due to social distancing, an overwhelming number of deaths globally, and an increase in unemployment. We are responding to some things that have been in place for a very long time—inequities based on race, class, gender identity, age, ability level, and citizenship. We are witnessing people who have been historically marginalized move further out in the margins with even less proximity to power.

If you are awake to what is happening at this time, you may be experiencing an enormous amount of sensitivity and heartbreak. A heart that is breaking and beating loudly as if to say, *Pay attention to what is going on!* Your heart might feel overcome with sensation while it responds to your nervous system's ringing of alarm bells throughout your entire body as a response to the cultural trauma and collective grief that surrounds. Your heart might feel tender as it tries to integrate all the experiences of collective trauma that could overwhelm your heart space. Trauma isn't innate to the heart; this is why the heart, in collaboration with the nervous system, continually attempts to move our self-system—the physical, emotional, mental, psychic, and spiritual parts of us—into balance by healing our trauma and processing our grief. As the heart brings our systems into greater balance, we begin to connect with our intuition and inner wisdom. This is a wisdom only the heart knows.

Many of us have been conditioned not to remember our intuition, inner wisdom, or the intelligence embedded in the heart. We have been conditioned to think our way through instead of feeling our way through. Dominant culture values the intellect more than our individual and collective intuition. The value of feeling our way through is that we can process what is present, making space to really listen to how our intuition wants to guide us.

In the 1970s, Dr. J. Andrew Armour introduced the "heart brain," positing the heart's intelligence as "the flow of awareness, understanding and intuition we experience when the mind and emotions are brought into coherent alignment with the heart."[*] The heart brain can be activated through consistent self-initiated practice. The more we bring our awareness to how the heart is guiding us, the greater our ability to access our intuition. Since the time of Dr. Armour's research, the heart brain has been studied extensively. What has been uncovered is that "the heart sends us emotional and intuitive signals that help govern our lives, the heart is in constant communication with the brain, the heart starts beating in an unborn fetus before the brain develops, the heart has its own extensive nervous system and the heart aligns many systems in the body so that they can function in harmony with one another."[†]

A strengthened relationship with one's heart begins to connect one with their inner wisdom and deep-knowing, supporting them in allowing their intuition to guide them as they respond to the things that break their heart, thus making space to grieve and heal. If we as a collective begin to engage our hearts' wisdom and inner-knowing, we can grieve and heal collectively. We will be able to create new ways of being that are not from our cultural

---

[*] "Heart Intelligence," HeartMath Institute, August 7, 2012, https://www.heart math.org/articles-of-the-heart/the-math-of-heartmath/heart-intelligence/.
[†] "Heart Intelligence," HeartMath Institute.

conditioning, but instead from our heart's intelligence. Our work is to develop a partnership with our hearts.

Anytime we respond to grief and loss, our nervous systems risk becoming overwhelmed. Our hearts risk becoming broken; instead of being in partnership with the heart, it can feel like we are at odds with it. At war with the heart. At times, we begin to move away from the heart's wisdom because it simply feels too difficult to connect with the sensation of being brokenhearted. When we are empathic, it can feel as if there is no separation between who we are and all that is happening around us. To continue to move through our lives with sensitivity and empathy in response to all that is happening to and around us, we need to create boundaries to maintain our energy and deepen our connection with our intuition and heart's wisdom.

Spiritual practice has supported me in doing both. If I am encumbered by all the noise in the world and the embodied overwhelm I feel in response to all that is heartbreaking, it is difficult to access my heart's wisdom and intuition. It is difficult to truly honor my intuition and how it wants to guide me. It is only through the practice of becoming still and quiet that I can notice, feel, process, and compost what needs to move through me while working to create healthy boundaries in relationships, with work, and with family members. When I can be still, bring energy back to myself, and remember my life force, my intuition will assist and guide me as I try to heal myself and create conditions to heal the collective. For me, healing often comes from remembering my true nature, which is inseparable from my intuition.

Spiritual practice is the anchor that grounds us. It is a consistent place we revisit for rejuvenation and a deeper relationship with ourselves and other sentient beings. Spiritual practice asks us to go inward and begin to understand that, while we have a relationship with the external world because we are in human bodies and part of what makes up the world, a connection with our internal experience might allow us to be guided in a way that better supports our collective healing.

There are many different ways to engage in spiritual practice, be it going inward by listening to the sound of the breath, engaging in a moving meditation, or engaging in mindfulness practices to aid us in beginning to notice patterns and behaviors that we might want to shift or transmute. When one is trying to create boundaries through spiritual practice, they can create an energetic field around themselves that still allows them to be in relationship with the outside world while also protected from the overwhelm of the outside world.

When one is working to connect with their intuition, they can ask to be in a relationship with their higher self—a self that is always available—to see if there is anything their higher self would like to communicate with them. They can ask questions when they are quiet and still, and wait for answers to come through in meditation, a sign or symbol from the natural world, or a sign from Spirit. The tools afforded to us through spiritual practice are endless; we just have to engage them.

Eric's passing made me face something I hadn't faced before: the loss of a dear friend. My process of grieving felt similar to the renovation our house was undergoing at the time. I felt my insides under construction. Everything inside was being shuffled and moved around. Just as Eric passed away, I was about to start yoga teacher training in the hopes of deepening my practice and offering yoga and mindfulness skills to clients in my psychotherapy practice. Eric's passing coinciding with the beginning of my yoga teacher training was not an accident; it was synchronous. When I signed up for teacher training, I had no idea how much the practice would deepen in its ability to hold my grief. Both my mat and cushion became receptacles for my grief.

My spiritual practice emerged as the space where I went to try to make sense of things that made no sense. I remember showing up on my yoga mat in countless classes and for yoga teacher training weekends to cry and mourn the passing of Eric. Sometimes, I would just sit on my mat and sob. At other times, I would feel Eric's energy guide me back into my heart and the knowing that our connection transcended the physical world. The practice of yoga stewarded me into moving with my grief. It supported me in making space for my grief without the process of grieving consuming me. The process of grieving can limit our energy, making it necessary for us to be mindful of how we use it. Yoga taught me how to work with my life force (prana) and to be discerning about where and how I choose to expend energy.

As I deepened my practice of yoga, the practice did what it is designed to do: it brought me back to my heart space and heart's wisdom. As I began to teach yoga, meditation, and mindfulness techniques, my connection with Eric in his afterlife and my ability to access my heart's wisdom and intuition increased. I began to embrace the intuition I have always embodied. I began to commune with nature—rivers, creeks, trees, animals, stones, and the elements—in a new way. I began to meditate as a way of connecting with Eric and those in different realms. I looked for signs and symbols representing my connection with Eric. I began to ask him for guidance and support. Eric was one of the first people I assigned the moniker "Spirit Guide."

Months after Eric's passing, his family and friends decided to create two memorials for him: placing a bench in the woods he loved so much and planting a tree in a different part of the woods. Both memorials landed at Bolin Creek, one on the Chapel Hill side of the creek and one on the Carrboro side.

The day I went to pick out the spot on the Chapel Hill side where the tree would be planted, I walked along the trail and I noticed two very large deer across the creek. They followed me along the trail—me on one side, them on the other—until we reached the perfect spot to plant the baby maple tree. I knew Eric's spirit was present in those deer and that he was with me and had a particular idea of where he wanted the maple tree to be planted.

The other memorial on the Carrboro side was a bench built by my friend, Kris. The bench was to be placed in Bolin Forest, a place Eric loved and knew well. We picked out a spot for the bench and engaged in a ceremony to honor Eric's life, and there is no doubt in my mind he was with us that day and every time I went back to visit the bench.

One day, I walked into the forest with the intention of visiting Eric's bench. I walked to where it had been located, but what I found was an empty space—no bench or evidence it had been there. The prior week, we had strong rains and the creek flooded. I assumed the bench washed away, but I couldn't find it anywhere. About a year later, Jeff and I were in the forest, making our way out of the woods, and we saw the bench sitting up high on a hill above the creek. Astonished, we wondered how a bench that was heavy and sturdy made its way a mile down the creek and up on a hill. Jeff took a picture of me sitting on the bench and we posted it on Facebook.

The response was immediate: "I know that bench. I've sat on it many times." "I saw that bench covered in debris in the creek." "I love that bench and have wondered where it went." One person responded and shared the story of finding the bench near its current location. He decided to pull it out of the creek and noticed a plaque on it that read:

Dear Life Traveler. Take a moment, and allow the sounds of nature to awaken your inner silence, and take you into your subconscious, where your deepest truths lie, love your life and its gifts. In honor of our dear friend, Eric Edwin Diener.

The man realized the bench was meaningful to someone and he dragged it up the hill above the creek so it would be safe from the rain and the risk of washing away. Eric moved his bench down a river and up on a hill where he wanted travelers to come and sit and view the water, listen to the wind and birds, and awaken their deepest truths, remembering to love their life and the gifts it offers.

On the day we spread his ashes at Graveyard Fields, we went on a long hike. And after hiking for a bit, I looked down on the ground and saw a heart-shaped rock looking back at me. I knew it was representative of Eric's heart, and it was special to hold it in my hand. It was a reminder that Eric's spirit was expansive. He was in the rocks, trees, stream, mountains, wind, and grass. He was everywhere. Today, that heart-shaped rock sits atop my ancestor altar.

Being connected to my intuition more deeply has led me to live my life from a place of listening to the natural world, which means I have had to acknowledge my connection with the natural world. Recognizing the connection I have with the planet calls me into behaving in a way that honors the planet. My ancestors have been available to communicate and work with me from a different realm; my work is to stay open as a channel for them to direct me as they sit in council and encourage me to live into what my highest self knows and desires. Eric reminds me to listen for the next step and for the information I need to know to inform the right next step, not just for myself but for humanity. My intuition reminds me of my divine connection with all energies, beings, and elements. When I see my own divine connection with other beings, I am able to lead my life in a way that is an attempt at living into the oneness of being instead of creating more suffering.

Intuition isn't just a thought; it's a feeling that comes from some other place than the intellect—a feeling that calls us into action. Now is a time when we desperately need to reconnect with our intuition and hearts' wisdom to steward ourselves and the planet into balance and a process of healing, just as my spiritual practice stewarded me in grieving the loss of Eric. We are born with a connection to our heart's wisdom. All we need to practice is remembering and nurturing this connection. The following practices are designed to teach you how to create boundaries and maintain your life force, as well as hear what your highest self and intuition have to communicate with you about what we as a collective need to do moving forward to live in more sustainable ways—ways that recognize our inherent resilience, wisdom, and connection.

PRACTICE
Sustaining Your Energy

For this practice, you will need your journal and pen or pencil. This practice will guide you through a meditation and a process to bring your energy back to yourself while staying connected to the external world. After the meditation, you will journal about the practice to create an imprint of your experience so you can bring your energy back to yourself whenever you need it.

We will start with a breathing practice to quiet your mind.

For this practice, I suggest you lie down or, if this posture doesn't resonate, then please find a different posture that would feel comfortable to you.

Close your eyes, soften your gaze, or find a grounding focal point and begin to breathe into your body. Start by taking deep breaths in and out. Begin to feel the shape change in your body as you breathe in and out. Notice the expansion as you breathe in and the contraction or release with your exhale.

If it feels okay, place your hand on your belly and a hand on your heart, and feel them move as you inhale and exhale.

Breathe for a few minutes here.

Notice the physical sensations and the emotions.

Now bring a color that represents healing into your awareness. Imagine there is a light around you—the color you've brought in is encompassing you. The light is limitless. As you are held and supported by the light, take a moment to ask for your energy to return to you so you can sustain your life force and strength. You can even say aloud, "I take my energy back now and I release any energy that isn't mine or is unhelpful." You can repeat this mantra several times.

After you have worked with the mantra, I invite you to notice how you feel physically, emotionally, mentally, and spiritually. Before transitioning out of meditation, take a moment to connect with your higher self and ask if there is anything your higher self wants to share with you. Listen deeply.

As you transition out of the meditation, thank the light and your higher self for aiding you in bringing your energy back to yourself.

Take a moment to invite in gentle movements and reawaken your body.

After the meditation, take a moment to reorient to your space. You can sit up, blink open your eyes, and notice any colors, shapes, or objects in your space.

Take a moment to journal about your experience of the color of the healing light, the practice of working to bring your energy back to yourself, connecting with your higher self, and any communication your higher self had with you, as well as what it was like to move out of the meditation. You can write, draw, or create art about your experience.

Lastly, come up with an image (abstract or representational) that will help you remember the experience of bringing your energy back to yourself.

PRACTICE

Connecting with Your Heart's Wisdom

For this practice, I suggest you go outside. You can go out into your yard, a favorite park or mountain, a garden, or whatever space in the natural world feels nurturing to you.

You will need space to move in some way, be it walking, sitting and swaying, standing, or stretching.

Once you have found your space, take a moment to settle into it. I invite you to notice the space you've chosen. Observe the colors, weather, flowers, trees, grass, clovers, stream, animals, and insects. Take stock of what is present in the environment you've chosen for this practice.

As you notice and observe the natural world, begin to notice your breath. Inhale and exhale.

Breathe here and be in communion with the natural world as a way of coming back to your heart's wisdom, true nature, and intuition.

See if you can synchronize your breath with some part of the natural environment. Can you inhale and exhale with the wind? Is it possible to inhale and exhale with the flow of the stream? Perhaps you can synchronize your breath with the animals, insects, or other energies around you. Take a few deep breaths.

Now I invite you to move, walk, sit and stretch, stand and stretch, kneel on the earth, walk barefoot on the earth—whatever movement your breath and consciousness are guiding you to engage in. Take at least five minutes to move intuitively in your body. Just let the breath and your connection with the earth allow you to move.

After five minutes, find stillness and either take a moment to connect to your heart, or place your right hand on your heart and your left hand on your right. Take a moment to check in with your heart's wisdom and with your nervous system. What does your heart have to share with you at this time?

Connect with your heart's wisdom as a way of connecting with your intuition, allowing it to assist you in governing your life from a place of deep wisdom and knowing. Stay here for as long as you would like, taking the time to be in the natural world and connect with your heart's wisdom.

When you are ready to transition, notice if there is an object from the natural world that makes sense to carry with you as you move forward. This object would be a totem to remember your experience, to remember that your heart always embodies wisdom, and to remember your intuition. A leaf, flower, acorn, hickory nut, a little water from the stream, a blade of grass, a four-leaf clover—whatever object speaks to you. When you approach the object, please ask permission to take it with you by simply asking if you can have it and then listening for the answer. Then take the object (if you hear a yes).

Now take some time to journal in response to the following questions:

- How did your experience with the natural world aid you in remembering your connection to all beings?
- How can a connection with your heart's wisdom via the natural world support you in taking actions in your life from a place of interconnectedness?

Ours is not the task
of fixing the entire
world all at once, but of
stretching out to mend
the part of the world
that is within our reach.

—Clarissa Pinkola Estés,
"Do Not Lose Heart; We Were
Made for These Times"

USHERING US

I hold so many warm memories of my grandmother, Dorothy, in my heart. When I was a little girl, I remember visiting her house every Sunday after church for family dinner. My brother, my mother, and I would sit around a big table filled with food, surrounded by aunts, cousins, and chosen family. We would fill ourselves with nourishment from the food and company. It was a ritual, which my grandmother loved. Her house and heart were warm. Family dinners and gatherings brought her joy.

One day, I was looking around in my grandmother's kitchen and discovered what looked like a shaker to make cocktails and mixed drinks. I asked my grandmother what it was, and it turned out to be an antique milkshake maker. Once my grandmother informed me of the real purpose of my discovery, I procured vanilla ice cream (my favorite) from her freezer and milk, wrapped a hand towel around the shaker, and began to make my milkshake. This became my ritual on Sundays, accompanying my grandmother's ritual of gathering us.

I have memories of spring at my grandmother's house and the purple hydrangea bush right outside the family room. It was vibrant, and when I was a little child, my perception was that the flowers seemed to be bigger than my head. My grandmother would let me clip one off of the bush and wrap a wet paper towel around it so it could travel safely home with me.

Right next to the hydrangea bush was a door that went into the back of the house. This is where my papa, Fred, used to spend most of his time. Papa was always kind to me, but I understood from my mother that, when she was growing up, he was an alcoholic. My mom shared about how the house could turn from a place of comfort to chaos within moments of her father, my papa, coming home from work. He would run my grandmother, my mom, and her two sisters out of the house. Apparently, when my brother and I were small children, my mother told Papa that he wouldn't be allowed to see us if he didn't stop drinking around us. He must have listened to her because we were able to continue to spend time with him.

Near the back door that led to where papa used to hide out is where my brother and I would play a game of stoplight with my cousins. When we got bored with the stoplight game, we would run around in the yard, make mudpies, and head back to the garden. My grandmother and Papa always had a big and flourishing garden. Although our generation never had an opportunity to experience the animals that accompanied their garden, my grandparents raised animals for food while my mother and two aunts grew up. We heard stories about the chickens, a duck, pigs, and a cow that lived on the land with them.

My grandparents had to grow and raise most of their animals for food because they grew up in the Jim Crow era. Papa worked odd jobs, on the railroad, in a chicken factory, and as a handyman, and Grandma worked for the Richmond Paper Company, and then as a domestic worker, cleaning people's homes. They grew and raised their food because they had to rely on themselves and the tight-knit Black community around them to survive. Although they were denied many opportunities such as voting rights, an equal education, and the ability to pass wealth on from one generation to the next, every time I was in their home, I felt like we had all we needed. They created conditions for their children, grandchildren, and great-grandchildren to thrive. They did this through their deep faith, determination, and resourcefulness.

My grandmother was the most devoted person I have ever known. She grew up in the church, which was the safe haven for many African American families suffering from systemic racism and injustice. The church was the place for organizing, grieving, ceremony, ritual, and rejoicing. I witnessed my grandmother "get happy" in church, moved by the spirit so much so that she couldn't stay seated in the church pew. She had to rise up and wave her hands, praising Jesus while the church ladies fanned her. Dorothy most certainly believed in God and Jesus Christ, and she had specific ideas about how to live a Christian life. She read her Bible every evening before bed. This was her spiritual practice. She explained away all the horrors of our world by saying, "God has a plan." She had faith, and her hope was to end up in heaven, free of her physical body to be with her mother, father, and other ancestors.

My grandmother's favorite holiday was Thanksgiving—everyone would come over to give thanks and gather, including the uncles, second cousins, grandkids, and all the people who didn't have any other place to go for a meal or the company of others. It is no surprise to me that my grandmother transitioned and began her journey to heaven the day before Thanksgiving. The timing of her stroke and passing caused many things to subsequently happen, one of which was gathering in her home for Thanksgiving dinner, eating at 10:00 p.m., and trying to enjoy the collards she had prepared for us. Even in her passing, she nourished us.

At the time of her passing, I was living in Portland, Oregon. I had planned to stay in Portland for Thanksgiving to be with friends, and then travel back to North Carolina and Virginia for Christmas. Instead, I traveled home to Virginia a few days before Thanksgiving so I could attend my dad's memorial, which his sisters had planned for the day before the holiday. I went to the memorial with my mother and aunt and saw people I'd never met and some that remembered me from when I was a child. I read the poem my aunts asked me to read and I listened as my cousins on my dad's side do what people so often do when someone who has lived a complex life passes away—uplift them with platitudes to make up for the shitty things they did while alive. My father abandoned us when I was two years old, and he treated my mother terribly over the years. He didn't show up as a father for my brother and me, and he didn't support us financially or emotionally. At times, I forgot I had a father.

As I sat in my seat for his memorial, making faces at my mom in response to something shared about him that was an absolute lie, I felt glad my father was no longer suffering. And I felt angry that people were lying about who he was—at least who he was to me, my mother, and my brother. At the memorial, my aunts came up to me and thanked me for reading the poem and being there. They hadn't spoken to me in years, had no idea what I did, where I lived, or what my life was like. They handed me a plaque with my father's name on it and then I left. My mother, aunt, and I went to my grandmother's house. She hadn't felt well enough to go to the memorial but did want to accompany us to Red Lobster for dinner. When my grandmother came out of the house, she looked a bit distressed and didn't have a coat on even though it was cold outside. My aunt Ethel made her go back in the house to get her coat, and I watched the role reversal of a child parenting their mother.

We went to dinner and had been seated for about ten minutes when my mom and aunt went to the restroom, leaving my grandmother and me at the table. I watched my grandmother pick up her knife and fork, trying to move them even though no food was on the table. She looked confused and I asked if she was okay. She couldn't talk. My mom and aunt came back from the restroom, saw that something was wrong, and immediately called for an ambulance.

The paramedics arrived and put my grandmother on a stretcher, asking her questions about her medication and what she had done that day. At one point, I heard her faint voice and then never heard her speak again. I rode in the ambulance with her because my mother's disability didn't allow her to get into the ambulance, and my aunt was busy calling my other aunt and cousins to inform them of what had happened, telling them to meet us at the hospital.

In the ambulance, two things occurred that I will never forget. The paramedic driving the ambulance looked at me and asked, "What did you do today?" to which I replied, "I went to my father's memorial." The ambulance driver looked how I felt, like this was unbelievable. I haven't heard of many people attending a memorial service for one of their parents preceding their grandparent having a stroke on that same day. Then I heard the paramedics in the back say, "Ms. Young, Ms. Young, stay with us." This is when I knew my grandmother was dying.

We arrived at the hospital, and they rushed my grandmother into a room where I accompanied her. My grandmother's eyes were closed, her lips tight, and she kept sitting up like she was fighting the situation at hand. While she wanted to go to heaven, she didn't want to die. Certainly not in this way. I held her hand as doctors and nurses buzzed around, taking blood pressure, doing scans, and asking me questions to which I didn't have answers. At one point I said, "She's a person, her name is Dorothy, and she is my grandmother." My desire was to have the medical professionals humanize her as she transitioned. We deserve to be humanized, especially as we are dying.

I held her hand as her body fought and I told her she could go. She was ninety-six years old, had lived a long and full life, and I wanted her to be at peace. She settled down and didn't move again. My mother and aunt made it to the hospital, and we tried to integrate what had just happened—a memorial for my father and the loss of the matriarch of our family.

My understanding of what happened is this: I believe my grandmother left her body while in the ambulance, when I heard the paramedics pleading for her to stay, but her physical body didn't perish until two days after her stroke. I am certain I was supposed to be there with her at the table when she first had the stroke. I am certain I was supposed to be with her in the ambulance and at the hospital before other family members arrived. She called me back home, and while it was via my dad's memorial, which was bizarre, I was there with her when she needed me. I wasn't scared of death or supporting her in transitioning. I was honored to witness her strong will and eventual surrender as she began her journey to heaven.

After my grandmother's funeral, my mother and I went to her house to clean out some things. My mother and grandmother were best friends, and I knew my mother was utterly heartbroken by the loss of her mother. I picked out some dishes and cups, searching for that old milkshake maker, but I couldn't find it. We made our way from the kitchen to the back of the house. We weren't going to go into the extra bedroom, but we felt called to enter it. We opened the door and then the closet.

It was as if Papa was leading me to a hidden treasure. When we opened the closet, we found a half-full handle of Dewar's Whiskey from 1980, some ammunition, my grandmother's old picnic basket, and the deed to the land my grandparents owned prior to purchasing the home my grandmother lived in until she transitioned. These did feel like hidden treasures.

We moved onto my grandmother's bedroom, which brought back memories of playing dress-up with her costume jewelry and adorning myself with the perfume that lived on her dresser. I saw her Bible on her nightstand and immediately went over and sat on her bed. I knew I wanted her Bible as a reminder of her deep devotion to God, and a reminder to always incorporate rituals into my life. We continued packing things up, and when we opened up her dresser, I saw her ushering gloves—just like the Bible, I knew they were meant for me. My grandmother was an usher in church and held that role with pride. I remember the white gloves, dress, tights, shoes, and hat that she wore while ushering church members to their seats. The ushers also sent around the collection plate, opened the church doors for the pastor to enter and exit, and generally ensured things were running smoothly during church services. Her gloves felt magical to me. Months later, a friend commented on the synchronicity of me wanting my grandmother's ushering gloves and me holding her hand and being with her when she was transitioning from her body.

Her gloves not only remind me of her devotion but also of the way she lived her life in service of others, which I am sure has everything to do with why I live my life in the way I do—in service of the collective good. After my grandmother transitioned, her presence from the spirit realm felt almost immediate to me. She quickly let me know she was an ancestor who was going to be present as I navigated my life. Her spirit felt expansive. I began to feel her everywhere.

Her presence feels different from other ancestors who have transitioned; her presence feels very close and often like energy residing behind my heart. Sometimes her hand is gently caressing me, and at other times, she is giving me a push or nudge. She is always ushering me, moving me in the right direction. Sometimes her energy feels as if it is all around me. Every time I lead a Dismantling Racism training or a *Skill in Action* workshop, my grandmother is with me. Her spirit recognizes the depth of my work and the risks I take as I raise consciousness about white supremacy, calling people into action. Often in these spaces, her energy fills the room, reminding me I am not holding the work of transformation on my own. She is with me. She is with us.

One day, two weeks prior to my mother's hospitalization, I was moving through a guided meditation and had an interesting experience with my grandmother. First, she came in as she often does and connected to my heart. Then her sister, Olivia, came, and then my great-grandmother, Angie, and several other women from my bloodline that are unknown to me. My grandmother brought the support circle of ancestors that day. Now, looking back, I wonder if she was preparing me for all that was to come in my mother's illness and near-death experiences. During the meditation, I felt held and nurtured, and I felt strong feminine ancestral support. The experience of being with my grandmother as she transitioned deepened my desire to engage my ancestors as allies and supports. Since that time, I have begun working with my ancestors in a more intentional way. I have held ceremonies and performed rituals for them, called their names into spaces, built ancestor altars, and communed with them in nature.

My grandmother had a hand in moving me across the country to Portland and in calling me home months later. She had a hand in my work expanding and my first book being successful. Although her nudging doesn't always make sense at the time, she nudges me to take risks that are in my highest good. My grandmother reminds me to sit in front of my altar and pray to decrease the suffering on this planet, my own suffering, and that of others. She speaks to me through feathers found on walks around cities across the globe. She gives very clear answers to me—*yes* or *no*. There is no *maybe* for her.

She makes things bloom for me, just like the beautiful hydrangea bush in her yard and the one that is now blooming in mine. She has shown me what it means to sacrifice, be strong, patient, steady, and vulnerable. This is how she was in her passing—she patiently waited until I came back home to Virginia to transition. She was so steady and strong in her passing and letting go of her physical body, and she allowed me to witness her in the most vulnerable act one can take: leaving this material, physical world. She taught me how to grieve the loss of my father, the loss of her, and the pain and heartache my mother felt in response to losing her best friend, her mother. She taught me how to grieve for the suffering in the world, and instead of shying away from what is truly breaking my heart and our collective hearts, she taught me to lean in and feel.

My grandmother lived a long life and, for the most part, she was happy. I did notice some grumpiness coming up for her as she aged—her body and arthritis made it difficult to be mobile and feel good in her body—but she persevered until the day she transitioned. I cannot imagine what it would be like to be in a body for ninety-six years, having weathered and delighted so much. After my grandmother's body stopped struggling in the hospital, she was peaceful and preparing for her journey to heaven. Being at peace when one dies makes the transition to the spirit world easier. Being at peace when one dies makes it easier to show up as a healthy and present ancestor.

One way we can cultivate peace while we are among the living is to be mindful about how we live our lives. We can practice being mindful in our relationships with other sentient beings and the planet, we can be mindful of how we honor the process of acknowledging suffering and grieving, and we can engage in the work we must do to decrease suffering and cultural trauma. My grandmother and our connection in the physical and spiritual world have strengthened my commitment to my dharma and the work of creating conditions for liberation for all on this planet. My grandmother has supported me in listening more deeply to myself—an extension of Eric's gift to me. As I have listened and attuned to what my ancestors want for me, where they want me to be located to do my work, and how they want to support me, I have received support in infinite ways.

We are in a time when many are contemplating their right role, location, responsibility, with whom to be in relationship, and how to sustain relationships across lines of difference. We are in a time of activated energy and global crisis. It is time to call on our ancestors to assist us in figuring out our right role and response to collective grief and cultural trauma as we strive to create conditions for collective healing. Our bloodlines and lineages can support us in being clear about and reckoning with where we come from and how we can show up in response to the pain and suffering cultivated by dominant culture—a culture that continues to fragment and ask us to withhold our emotional response to collective trauma and grief.

Social location is important when one considers what their role might be. Social location is connected to your social group membership, identities, and points of privilege and oppression.

As a living ancestor, you embody points of privilege based on the identities that dominant culture deems as "normal and good," and points of oppression based on the identities that dominant culture deems as "abnormal and bad." For example, certain identities, such as white, male, heterosexual, able-bodied, thin or athletic body type, Christian, and many others, have proximity to power. This is a power to move freely, breathe, not live paycheck to paycheck, be able to legally get married or adopt children, practice a faith tradition safely and without ridicule, and not have to consider how you will navigate spaces because of your physical abilities. Dominant culture positions us either close to power or further away from power, based on the identities we embody. Given this reality, and as we lean into the call to grieve and change, we have different roles and responsibilities.

I am a cisgender, Black, heterosexual, middle-class, able-bodied woman with a master's degree. Being Black feels most salient to me as an identity and gives me much less proximity to power than white people. Being able-bodied and heterosexual gives me closer proximity to power. I am uniquely positioned to make change and have a specific role in responding to the trauma and subsequent grief that arises from a culture that gives and takes away power based on identity. This awareness is what led me to live into my dharma of teaching about dismantling racism and oppression in spiritual spaces. Even deeper than awareness, my connection with my grandmother and ancestors led me to identify the healing that needs to happen for me to tend to my racial trauma and any cultural conditioning that comes out of the experience of being oppressed.

My grandmother, and the ancestors within my bloodline, remind me of the trauma of what it means to be in a Black body, embodying an experience and memory of being enslaved alongside the resilience of my people, Black people. We have survived so much and, even as white supremacy tries to make us cease to be, we continue to persist. If, in my persistence and attempt to thrive, I am only focused on my Blackness and not the other identities I embody, especially the privileged ones, then I cannot effectively live into my right role. I need to heal from the violence dominant culture perpetuates based on race and look at my other points of oppression and privilege. One example of this might be me working in solidarity with Black trans people living with disabilities who are also experiencing houselessness as I seek to create conditions for liberation and provide spaces for people to grieve and heal. I need to advocate and be in relationship and solidarity with the people who are further out in the margins—those who have less proximity to power.

Right role and response will shift based on the cultural context. For example, prior to the 2020 murders of Breonna Taylor,

Tony McDade, Ahmaud Arbery, and George Floyd and countless others who didn't make the national news, some white people and many BIPOC were aware of policing and, in particular, how policing has been used to control Black bodies and bodies of color. This awareness led folks to lobby for police reform, raise awareness about police brutality, and think more critically about what it means to show up in solidarity, allowing Black people who are deeply affected by police brutality to center their experiences and lead movements such as Black Lives Matter. After the deaths of so many Black bodies during a global pandemic, the cultural context shifted and prompted a global uprising centered on how devalued Black people have been as a result of white supremacy. These are two different points in history, pre-uprising and in the middle of the uprising, which means how we show up may shift based on the moment, the context, and what is needed.

It is critical to ask for support and guidance from our ancestors as we meet the moment and as we position ourselves to respond to cultural trauma. We are encountering centuries of ancestral trauma, grief, anger, rage, sadness, resilience, perseverance, confusion, and pain. Ancestors can provide support to us because, while we are situated differently based on our social locations, our ancestry and histories are intertwined. Our traumas and what needs to be grieved are intertwined. Our ancestors have experienced wars, plagues, white supremacy, and systems of dominance. Our ancestors have lived during times of colonization, being stolen, land-stealing, caste systems, and segregation. In our bloodlines, there is wisdom about how to respond to what is happening to us and our planet. This wisdom propels us into our heart space. It is a wisdom that is old and deep, bigger than any one moment. Our practice of responding to what is breaking our hearts needs to involve us engaging our ancestors as we move through the history of what they lived and created. We must grieve and envision new ways of living.

There can be uncertainty when one begins to work with their ancestors because so many of our bloodlines embody deep trauma, legacies of oppression, suppression, violence, and harm. There is no way to engage with our ancestors without encountering history and how we, as people who make up communities and cultures, haven't chosen to reconcile, repair, or acknowledge how harm has happened throughout our collective history. By working to heal our bloodlines, we work to heal ourselves and future generations.

If you are just beginning to work with your ancestors, I encourage you to only invite in ancestral energy that will support your highest good. Ask for ancestors who are healthy and well to support you. If you find it difficult to engage with people in your bloodline, you might consider engaging the natural world as a living ancestor. Sometimes, it is easier to work with elemental energies because air, fire, water, earth, ether, and wood are things many of us have access to in some form. These elements are a reminder of the dynamic nature of the earth, always trying to come back into balance to further support the ecosystem that inhabits it.

As you begin your work to heal your trauma, healing will happen in your bloodline, which is in service of the collective's highest good. Healing is a process. Working with our ancestors can take time and patience. Finding our right role and a way to respond to the immense amount of grief and trauma, while remembering our resilience, is a process. Healing comes from the process of grieving in response to our traumas. My connection with my ancestors has taught me how to show up because they show up for me, guiding me on my path. They insist I work to heal myself and they let me know they are here with me, supporting me in the process of healing. When we engage the medicine that comes from acknowledging ancestral wounds and resilience, while also committing to explore and embody our right role in response to the cultural context, we can heal.

PRACTICE

Calling in Ancestral Support

In preparation for working with your ancestors and calling in ancestral support, I suggest you create a sacred space, either inside or outside, to connect with your ancestors.

To prepare a space, you might build an altar or place some meaningful objects around you on a table or in your hands. If you're setting up a sacred space outside, you can build an altar from found objects. You might choose to call in a specific ancestor or call in general ancestral support and guidance.

As part of your preparation, please meditate on or journal about the following questions:

- How do I feel about calling in and receiving ancestral support?
- What am I seeking in connecting more deeply with my ancestors?
- Is there anything I fear about connecting with my ancestors?
- What is my greatest hope for developing a relationship with my ancestors?

Take some time and work with these questions for as long as you would like. This is a good beginning to think about ancestor work.

Meditation: Calling in Ancestral Support

For this practice, you will be guided to cultivate a relationship with your ancestors and gain clarity about your right role, based on your social location, through exploring where you come from. You will move through a meditation and then journal about your experience. You can choose to meditate wherever feels most comfortable to you.

Find a comfortable way to be, either sitting, standing, or lying on your back, and make sure you are well-supported. You can support yourself with a blanket or pillow, or by placing a comforting object nearby.

Once you have found a comfortable way to be in your body and feel well-supported, close your eyes, soften your gaze or find a grounding focal point, and begin to breathe into your body.

Start by taking deep breaths in and out. Begin to feel the shape change in your body as you breathe in and out. Notice the expansion as you breathe in and the contraction or release with your exhale.

Breathe for a few minutes here.

Notice the physical sensations and the emotions.

Your breath is preparing you to connect with your ancestors—the people and places from which you come. You have complete agency during this meditation. If considering your family of origin brings up any trauma or unsettles the nervous system, you can connect with the earth or the cosmos—both are ancestors and places from which we all emerge.

Now begin to trace back in your mind to the people, spaces, and memories connected to the place you come from. You might begin to see people's faces. Memories might start moving through your mind. Family stories and rituals might flow through your consciousness. As you sift through what is arising in your consciousness, take a moment to call in ancestral support.

You can do this by saying, "I call in all well and healthy ancestors to support me at this time." You can repeat this to yourself several times. Take a moment to notice how you feel.

You can pause the practice here, perhaps taking a moment to journal and come back to it again later. In this next part of the practice, you will call on your ancestors to share wisdom about your right role based on your social location.

When you are ready, ask your ancestors to share some wisdom that will support you in responding to the present moment and the grief that needs to move through you. When you ask for wisdom from them, you might begin to notice images, colors, shapes, people, or memories arising in your consciousness. Ask them to share about how you might respond in this moment based on your social location and on the wisdom in your bloodline or ancestry. Ask them to share with you about your right role, based on your social location, in responding to the present cultural context. You can begin to ask your ancestors to give you information about your role, response, and the resources you need to respond. Take as long as you would like. Once you are ready to move out of this part of the meditation, take a few deep breaths. Reground in your physical space and journal about your experience.

In journaling, consider writing about any healthy ancestors that came through as well as any guidance they offered to you about your role and social location. This is a meditation you can revisit over and over as it might take time to connect with your ancestors. Remember you can connect with the earth as a living ancestor if your own ancestral lineage isn't coming through to meet you. I suggest you practice this meditation once a week. Any more than that could overwhelm your nervous system as you might be trying to force a connection with your ancestors. They are present and you are working on developing a relationship with them. Please take your time and be gentle with yourself and with them. This is a new relationship, and it takes time to build trust in relationships.

● ● ●

OTHER IMPORTANT THINGS TO CONSIDER WHEN WORKING WITH ANCESTORS

If you are new to working with your ancestors or already have a regular practice, there are a few things to consider as you develop or deepen your relationship.

Reciprocity

It is important to have an ongoing relationship with your ancestors, and one that isn't just about you asking for their support, but also a relationship where you are giving to them. As you consider how you might give back to your ancestors for their support, think about what they liked to eat, the music they enjoyed, or sayings they used to say.

For example, my grandmother loved wine on Thanksgiving. And she used to always say, "It's so quiet in here" as we ate our Thanksgiving dinner, because "the food is good" and we were all too busy chewing to talk. She loved sweet potato pie and sherbet. She loved to garden, and she loved her great-grandchildren and her grandchildren. When I make offerings to her, I make sure to prepare a plate for the altar and a little shot glass of wine, and I talk to her as I am making an offering. This is my way of thanking her for offering her undying ancestral support.

You want to let your ancestors know you are supporting them as well—this is about healing your bloodline, lineage, and yourself. Reciprocity is part of what makes healing occur. Reciprocity honors the relationship you have with people who have transitioned and maintains balance so that your relationship isn't based on your asking or taking, but on your giving and receiving.

Maintaining a Relationship with Your Ancestors

Ancestors are present to offer us support as we move through our lives and prepare for our own transitions. It is important to stay in relationship with them. You might build an ancestor altar with things your ancestors loved, like my grandmother's ushering gloves, or pictures, or meaningful objects. You can develop an ongoing practice of sitting in front of your ancestors and being with their energy. You might have conversations with your ancestors or write notes to them. Stay in relationship with them in whatever way feels meaningful and purposeful to you.

And remember, the earth is a living ancestor and there are many ways to connect with the earth. Take a walk, thank the animals when they cross your path, breathe in fresh air, and watch for synchronicities in nature. There are endless possibilities when it comes to asking the earth, our living ancestor, for support.

A hive is wholeness. One bee experiences all that every bee experiences. There is no separation. Whereas you have separation, we are born into a world beyond the borders of singularity. Our first thought is always of the hive, to bear increase in the world as we sing the world into aliveness.

—Jacqueline Freeman,
Song of Increase: Listening to the Wisdom of Honeybees for Kinder Beekeeping and a Better World

THE HIVE MIND

I found myself staring at a receipt on the computer screen, wondering what I had just done.

I must have awoken from a dream and felt the divine call to purchase bees because the receipt that was staring back at me indicated I had ordered two packages of bees, bee boxes, and all the hive components one needs to begin keeping bees. It was 5:00 a.m. in the morning in early May 2019, and although I had already moved back to North Carolina from Portland, I still had work projects there. I was visiting Portland to work with a client, and I was managing my mother's care from afar. To say I was stressed would be an understatement. I was completely overwhelmed, trying to maintain some of my professional commitments, continue to make enough money to pay my mortgage, and take care of my mother. I was moving through one of the most stressful points in my life, which didn't seem like the optimal time to become a beekeeper without knowing anything about bees. But some beekeepers believe bees choose us, and in my case, they definitely did.

I stared at the receipt and immediately texted two of my friends who are beekeepers. I was panicking at this point, unsure of what I would do when the bees arrived. Both friends replied and offered to support and help me as I endeavored to become a beekeeper.

After waiting two weeks for the bees to arrive, I received a voicemail from the post office, telling me to come and get my bees. There was an urgency in their message, and when I went to retrieve the bees, I understood why. A postal worker went to the back to get the bees and came out with two screened boxes, each containing around ten thousand bees. They were buzzing about, and with trepidation, the postal worker handed them over to me as everyone else in the post office looked at me with curiosity and confusion. I drove home with the bees buzzing in my backseat, having no idea how to place them in the hives I had prepared. I called a friend, who talked me through the process as I successfully hived both packages of bees.

When you receive a new package of bees, along with them comes a queen assigned to them, but this is not a queen who the hive designated for themselves. It takes a few days for them to get used to the queen's pheromones. If the queen is released too quickly, the hive might reject her. Bees use chemical cues to communicate. The hive and different types of bees respond to signals emitted by different kinds of pheromones that determine when and how they defend the colony, mate, produce eggs, and forage. During the process of hiving bees, you place them in the hive with frames for them to begin building honeycomb, and you place the queen cage (a tiny screened box with a queen and a few worker bees) in between two frames or on top of the frames. One end of the queen cage has a cork, and the other end has candy. The candy is crystallized sugar that ensures the queen stays in the cage until it is time for her to be released. While the bees work to release the queen from her cage, they feed her and give her water to ensure she is nourished and sustained while waiting to be released. Once she is released, she begins laying eggs to support the growth of the colony.

After setting up the hives, I placed an extra box on top of the hive cover to feed the bees. It isn't standard practice to feed hives, except when you first get them and during the dearth season, when there is far less nectar flowing in the heat of summer in the Western hemisphere.

I was so curious about the bees. I likely went into the hive a bit too much at the beginning. I learned this is common for new beekeepers. I was fascinated with the new energy in my yard and environment, and I began going out to feed them each day for a month. I stood near their hives, watching them buzz in and out, and I went into the hive to make sure there was brood, eggs, larvae, and pupae of honeybees. It was exciting to learn more about a bee's process to support the collective good of the entire hive.

While I was forging a new relationship with my hives, whom I named Sting and the Spice Girls, I continued to be overwhelmed by my mother's illness and her declining health. For the first two months of tending the bees, I was also tending my mother, managing her care as she moved in and out of hospitals and skilled nursing facilities. Curious about the mystery of bringing bees into my life during such a stressful time, I reached out to one of my friends, Karla (a bee priestess and healer), and asked her what she thought about the timing of it all. She informed me that bees are psychopomps. I had no idea what this meant. She went on to explain that bees move between the material and spirit worlds. Karla believed they came to me because they were assisting my mother as she contemplated her transition from the material to spirit world.

The word *psychopomp* originates in Greek mythology. *Pomp* means "guide" or "conductor" and *psyche* is one's breath, life, soul, and mind. Psychopomps are guides who lead people through the transition from life to death and the afterlife. In Greek mythology, bees were associated with the souls of the dead. Some Greek philosophers believed humans could be reincarnated as bees, or that the bees were souls of those who had not yet been born. The bees had indeed come to support my mother in her transition, and to bring sweetness and energy to me as I felt the gravity of what it might be like for my mother to transition and no longer be here with me in her physical form.

As the summer progressed, my relationship with the bees deepened, and this was when I received my first sting. I was inspecting one of my hives and must have been hastily making my way through the frames. As I was holding a frame full of bees, I felt a burning sensation in my right thigh. I screamed, not really sure what was happening to me. I held onto the frame of bees and looked down to see a stinger in my thigh. After a bee sting, the venom continues to release until you pull the stinger out. I closed up the hive, came into my house, pulled out the stinger, and sat there perplexed about what had caused the bee to sting me.

After about ten minutes, I remembered that many people who believe in the mysticism of bees say you only get stung where you need to be stung—they say the venom is medicine. I accepted this belief as true. Since puberty, I have struggled with a similar condition to the one my mother has—lymphedema, swelling of the limbs. My legs swell and feel inflamed much of the time. Hormonal imbalances seem to have something to do with this condition, although my mother's may have been a vascular issue. Being stung in the right thigh may have been the bee's way of offering medicine to me to decrease inflammation in my legs and promote healing in my body. It took some time to feel the effects of the medicine, yet I have noticed a decrease in flare-ups of lymphedema since being stung.

I began to read books, take online courses about bee mysticism, and soak up as much information as I could about bees. I sat out next to the hives, meditating and doing magic. I watched the bees pollinate my garden, and I had the best crop of tomatoes, cucumbers, and zucchinis I have ever had. I carefully walked through the clover in my yard, pausing to watch the bees gather pollen to take back to the hive and store it until it would be used to produce honey. I learned about the various roles that bees have within the hive. The queen bee is the only fertile female in the bee colony. She is the only one who can lay fertilized eggs. The queen emits pheromones only detectable by the bees to let her hive know she is alive and well.

Drones are male honeybees and one of their main tasks is to fertilize new queens. They do not have stingers and cannot participate in protecting the hive. Instead, they keep the brood warm. Their bodies aren't constructed in a manner that allows them to collect pollen. Some honey bee colonies kick out the drones in the fall, when food within the colony begins to become limited. Drones are the only bees that can visit other hives to carry the song of their hive into another hive. When they enter other hives, they walk past the guards and into the brood chamber to warm the brood.

Worker bees are the largest population in the bee colony, and they are all females. Each worker, guided by a biological clock, assumes different job responsibilities. As they age, their job function and duty might change. The cleaners clean the cells in the honeycomb, preparing them for the queen to lay eggs in them. The nurse worker bees attend to the developing larvae, and it is believed nurse bees check on a single larva at least one thousand times a day—true commitment to the developing larvae. They feed the queen larva as well as the drone larva. If the hive is infected with a parasite like the varroa mite, the nurse bees selectively eat honey that has a high antibiotic level to then share it with other bees within the colony. As the worker bees age, they serve as undertakers, carrying the dead bodies of bees out and as far away from the hive as possible. If there is brood that is dead or diseased, the undertakers will also carry these out to ensure the health of the colony.

At twelve days old, worker bees can begin to build honeycomb by secreting and producing beeswax. The temperature of the hive is very important, and some worker bees serve as temperature controllers. When it is warm in the hive, the temperature controllers gather water, bringing it back to the hive to spread it on the backs of the bees who are fanning. Bees ventilate the hive by fanning their wings, bringing the temperature down with evaporated water. When it is cold in winter, these worker bees congregate as a cluster to keep the hive warm. Becoming a guard of the hive means a worker bee is close to assuming the role of forager.

Guard bees protect the hive. The guards inspect every bee as it returns to the hive to make sure it belongs to the colony. They do this by making sure the bees returning to the hive have a familiar scent. Guard bees also protect the hive from robbers that might come from other bee colonies, as well as other insects.

Foragers leave the hive at sunrise in search of pollen, water, nectar, and propolis. They make about ten trips a day, each lasting about an hour. Assuming the role of forager means a bee is in the last stage of its life. When nectar is flowing, many foragers die in the field. As fall approaches winter, much less foraging happens, and foragers tend to die in the hive.

As foragers gather pollen, a vital resource for the hive, they pollinate many of our crops, providing fresh food to us for our sustainability and health. Honeybees pollinate almost 90 percent of the world's crops. Every time you eat an apple, a peach, an almond, or a cherry, you are eating the fruits of the labor of bees. Many of us have become accustomed to eating fresh fruit and vegetables, but without bees pollinating them, they would not be readily available and the price of these items would increase.

People with higher incomes and closer geographic proximity to organic food co-ops and farmers markets may continue to have access to fresh fruits and vegetables because of their proximity to power and willingness to pay a bit more for food that should be accessible to everyone. An increase in the prices of fresh vegetables and fruit would deeply affect access for those who are already suffering economically and are marginalized because of systemic oppression. A lack of healthy foods, coupled with systemic oppression, is linked to disparate health outcomes for communities who are underestimated, low-wealth, and of color.

As I gained knowledge about the various roles of bees within colonies, I was struck by how each role is for the good of the hive. Bees do not see themselves as individuals; they see themselves as an extension of the hive—a collective unit whose goal and purpose are to ensure the health of not only the hive while they are alive and part of it but also the future generations of bees that will continue their legacy of collective care. As summer transitioned to fall, I felt nervous about preparing the hive for winter. I wasn't sure if they had enough honey stores to make it through the season, but alongside my nerves, the hives were preparing as well. In the fall, the queen bee begins to diminish egg production but does lay brood, which becomes winter bees. Instead of living the normal life cycle of a bee, which lasts six to eight weeks, the winter bees live up to six months to ensure the hive can make it through winter and emerge in spring.

That year, it became very cold in late November in North Carolina, and I decided to place candy boards (wood frames filled with sugar, protein, and carbohydrates) in the hives to make sure they had enough food. One of the main reasons bees do not survive winter is starvation. I sealed up the hives, making a commitment to stay out of them to allow the bees the opportunity to better control the temperature of the hive and cluster to keep themselves warm.

During late fall and winter on sunny days, I would see bees come in and out of the entrance, but I also began to see dead bees around the hive. This worried me, and I read many blogs about what it means if you see more dead bees around the hive in the winter. When it's warm outside in spring or summer, bees usually die in the field while they are foraging; if they do die in the hive, the undertakers carry them out, disposing of their bodies. During wintertime, bees die in place—they die at home, in the hive, which would explain the dead bees around the hive entrance because undertakers cannot carry out dead bodies if it's below 40 degrees Fahrenheit. I was relieved when I read this information.

One day, I was out near the Spice Girls' hive when I noticed a bee emerge and lock eyes with me before it took off from the landing board. I thought it was odd that it looked my way and lingered for a moment, but I also thought maybe it was just a bit slower that day. Looking back, now I know the bee was giving me a look of concern. The imprint of that bee's gaze stayed with me until two weeks later when I awoke from a dream about the bees. In the dream, I was in a large room that had a terrarium inside it. The room was dimly lit, there was a long table with frames from the beehive on it, and bees were flying around inside the terrarium. I and whoever was in the dream with me were inspecting the frames when we noticed honey and some brood. I remember feeling confused about why the frames were outside of the hive and why we were inspecting them.

I looked over to the terrarium and saw bees building honeycomb. But instead of building it in a row to store eggs, brood, pollen, and honey, they were building structures that hung down from the ceiling of the terrarium, resembling the structure of a sweet gumball. Except they weren't spiky on the edges—they were smooth. I thought it was odd they were building honeycombs in this way and that the structures weren't connected—they were separate with bees on each of them.

I was mesmerized by these shapes in the dream. As I stared at them with wonder, they transformed into deep-purple flowers resembling morning glories. I was stunned by the beauty of the flowers and the bees pollinating them. Morning glories are associated with witchcraft, specifically as an aid to support divination and astral travel. After watching this resplendent sight, I walked outside into the sunlight and then awoke from my dream. The dream stayed in my psyche for two weeks. I knew something was wrong with the hive, but I didn't want to go into it by myself—I knew I would feel devastated if one of the hives was dead.

On December 23, 2019, my mother was rehospitalized due to another infection or an extension of the original one she had in April 2019. Perhaps it didn't truly heal. It can take a long time to heal a powerful infection. Once again, I was traveling back and forth to Richmond, trying to make sure my mother was being cared for by a system not designed to center her care. I was afraid the same thing was happening all over again—that my mother, my ancestral root, would receive inadequate care, institutional racism would cause her needs to be made invisible, and because of this, death would meet her and take her away from the material world.

When I would visit my mother, she was not herself; she didn't recognize me and became very irritable and angry. I don't blame her for being angry and I believe even through her confusion and lack of lucidity, she knew her needs weren't being met by the health-care system. I was overwhelmed with the same things I had been overwhelmed by when I first purchased the bees: my mother's health, how to sustain my work while caring for my mother; how to sustain my physical and mental health; how to maintain enough energy and stamina to drive back and forth from North Carolina to Richmond to make sure her needs were met; and the knowledge that if I wasn't with my mother twenty-four hours a day, watching what the doctors and nurses were doing or not doing, my mother's chances of survival were slim. I was holding this overwhelm and the looming thought that something might be wrong with the Spice Girls.

On December 30, 2019, my partner, Charles, and I went up to the hive, and it was quiet. No buzzing nor evidence of life. We opened the hive and didn't see any bees until we moved into the brood chamber and caught a glimpse of the bottom board, which was covered with dead honeybees. There are no words for what it is like to see a once alive-and-thriving hive lifeless. My heart began to hurt so intensely. Charles supported me in clearing off the bottom board and we began to go through each frame to find out what happened. They had enough food because they had a full box of honey and an untouched candy board. We couldn't figure out what happened, but our best guess is that water got into the hive and the bees weren't able to dissipate it and stay warm, while temperatures outside became cold. The bees could have frozen to death. The truth is we won't ever know what happened to the hive. I felt like a terrible beekeeper and person because I let one of my hives die. The Spice Girls would no longer be able to support their hive and the earth in the myriad ways honeybees do, and I felt responsible for their deaths. As we moved through each frame in the hive, we were met with what beekeepers call "a super": an entire medium-sized box of honey. It was capped with wax and we could see the golden honey underneath it. When I first started keeping bees, I was not intending to harvest honey. I wanted to leave all of it for them. But there we were faced with a full box of honey and no hive to eat it. I had none of the tools one might need to harvest honey, but Charles is a professional chef with MacGyver-like skills, and we knew he could think of a way for us to harvest the honey with tools in my kitchen.

We gathered up our tools: a sharp knife, colander, cookie sheet, cheesecloth, and mixing bowl. We set up in my garage with the frames of honey and began the harvest. Charles used the knife to cut the wax cap off the frame, exposing shiny, delicious, golden honey. I scraped the honey from the frames and into a colander, and then watched the honey slowly drain into the mixing bowl. Our fingers, hands, and clothing were sticky with sweet honey. We spent hours harvesting the honey and were finally able to place it in mason jars.

It was a process that required time and mindfulness. I was struck by the bees leaving us a gallon of honey in their passing.

The juxtaposition of so much sweetness and the tragic death of the colony was almost too poetic. In the next box—the brood box—we saw brood, larva, pupating and capped-over, waiting to emerge from their cell. We saw pollen and bees stuck to frames, some with their heads in cells and butts sticking out, and some hanging onto the frames. We discovered one frame that held the queen's body and worker bees surrounded her. I believe the worker bees were trying to keep her warm and protected until their final moments together. They labored to protect their queen and hive because, without a queen, the hive cannot sustain itself. I felt this on a sensory level—what it might be like to protect your beloved queen to ensure the health of the hive. I was curious about the queen's last moments and if she was aware the hive was trying to protect her until the hive transitioned to the spirit realm. I imagine so.

The offering of sweet honey amid death and loss, along with caring for the queen and colony until its passing and death, deeply touched me. The contiguity of sweetness and death made me think back to what Karla shared with me when my mother was first hospitalized for an infection: "They came to you because they are assisting your mother as she contemplates her transition from the material to spirit world." For days after discovering the colony had died, I prayed to the bees and thanked the colony for its life. On the surface, the bees appeared to have frozen to death, and on an energetic and spiritual level, I believe the colony sacrificed itself and traveled to the spiritual realm through honeycomb and with the assistance of morning glories so my mother could stay in the material world for a bit longer. Since their transition, and whenever I eat the honey they left us, I am thankful for their mysticism and alchemy. I am grateful for the sustenance the Spice Girls provided in so many ways, the gift of still having my mother here in physical form, and for the hive's constant reminder of the necessary and vital practice of collective care.

As bee colonies pollinate our food, bless this earth, and support us through their work of being in the spirit and material realms, they are facing devastating concerns that could lead to colony collapse. Parasites, pesticides, and stress on the colonies due to the commercialization of agriculture, starvation, and climate change are all factors that place bee colonies at risk. Honeybees support the growth of trees, flowers, and other plants, which serve as sustenance for us along with providing shelter for small beings who are part of the ecosystem. Our ecosystem is well-designed, but fragile and vulnerable. One shift in it can shift everything.

The ocean warming due to increasing greenhouse gas emissions because of human behavior is causing coral bleaching and the loss of marine life breeding grounds. Humans and other beings are at risk of losing their main food source—fish and marine mammals. Climate change affects our forests by placing them more at risk for wildfires, pest outbreaks, droughts, and slowing plant growth. These risk factors can lead to a change in ecological relationships. Abruptly changing the health of the forest negatively affects wildlife and human systems. In addition, greenhouse gases create climate change, trapping heat in the atmosphere and contributing to respiratory issues such as asthma, allergies, and cardiovascular diseases.

We are suffering from the amnesic state that dominant culture has created, causing us to disassociate from our true nature and the reality that *we are nature*. We suffer due to systems of oppression that set up paradigms based on the premise that some members of our hive and collective are worthy of life and care, while others are disposable. We are facing devastating concerns that could lead to the collapse and dismantling of our humanity. Dominant culture strips us of the memory that we are part of a collective hive, which serves as an extension of a larger organism and encourages us to take action in service of the whole. Dominant culture makes us forget what it means to practice caring for the whole rather than our individual needs and wants. This includes not only other humans but also the natural world, honeybees, and all parts of our ecosystem.

The practice of collective care for other beings and the ecosystem is not new. Many communities that have been marginalized due to systemic oppression have been in the practice of collective care out of necessity. Many communities that have been marginalized and underestimated have had to take care of their own needs, and many have been conditioned to see themselves as part of the hive because of their awareness that dominant culture affects them in similar ways. Communities that have been underestimated have had to learn how to be creative and revolutionary, remembering their own resilience as an act of sustaining their survival. We are living during a time where it is important for us all to embrace the practice of collective care. We are living during a time where remembering we are precious to one another and remembering that all parts of our ecosystem are precious to us might allow us to heal the fragmentation that comes from living in a culture that doesn't allow us to be whole or see ourselves as part of the whole.

While the honeybees have taught and continue to teach me so much about what it means to be in communion with other beings and to uphold them as being cared for as much as I extend care to myself, they have also taught me about what it can look like for a hive to thrive. After the Spice Girls transitioned, their space in the beeyard was vacant for three months. Sting, the other hive, continued to show signs of life prior to Charles and me opening it after winter transitioned into spring. I felt timid about opening Sting, but I could hear buzzing and saw a few bees near the entrance—all signs they successfully made it through winter. We opened the telescoping cover and saw bees on top of the hive cover. I didn't want to turn the bottom side of the hive cover toward myself because my sense was there were thousands of bees on it. The look on Charles's face confirmed this feeling.

I went to place the hive cover down on the ground and discovered it was covered with buzzing bees. The bees had filled up the frames in their brood box and they filled the frames in the medium box that sat atop the brood box. On top of the frames, they had built honeycomb in a spiral shape. The comb was full of drone eggs. My being a new beekeeper meant I didn't see all the signs indicating the colony had run out of space in the hive over winter.

When bees run out of space, they prepare to swarm, carrying at least half the hive with them to create an extension of the existing colony in a different space. We removed the comb that was on top of the frames, added another medium box, and then replaced the hive cover and telescoping lid, closing up the hive. I was thrilled there were so many bees and that they had made it through winter. That same day, Charles and I brought a new hive home. We set them up in what had been the Spice Girls' hive, and we made sure they were fed with a special medicinal tea made up of chamomile, yarrow, stinging nettle, peppermint, echinacea, sage, hyssop, thyme, and lemon balm. It took weeks to figure out what to name the new hive and then it came to me: Infinity would be their name, in honor of the Spice Girls and the ongoing nature of their energy and spirit.

The following weekend, I was in my kitchen and heard an unfamiliar buzzing sound. It sounded like thousands of bees were buzzing next to my kitchen window. I looked outside and saw more bees than I have ever seen. I watched, unsure if I was supposed to be alarmed as I watched the bee show that blazed across the sky. I walked out to Sting's hive and it was abuzz. I could tell something was shifting, but again, I had no idea the hive was swarming. I watched the sky, bees darting everywhere. It felt like a festive occasion. I estimated twenty thousand bees were in the swarm that emerged from the hive that day. After watching them for a few minutes, they all returned to the hive. They hung on the outside of the hive, buzzing and vibrating the beeyard.

The next day, I was on the phone with Sara, a local beekeeper and member of the Triad Beekeepers Association, to inquire about what I had experienced with the bees the day before. Suddenly, I heard the buzzing again. Sara was explaining I had indeed witnessed a swarm. She shared that when the bees swarmed on the previous day, the queen must not have left with them and this is why they returned to the hive. The buzzing became louder and louder, and I told Sara it appeared they might be swarming again. I quickly jumped off the phone and went out in the beeyard.

I saw a similar sight to the one I had seen the day before—bees filling up the sky, buzzing loudly. They landed on a tree branch that hung above my fence. I watched as they clung on, making the tree branch heavier and heavier. I was captivated by the experience. This happened during the COVID-19 outbreak, and I knew it would be difficult to find someone to remove them and place them in a new hive for me to add them to my set of bee colonies. If someone would have been able to come out and remove them, I would have ended up with two colonies from Sting, the original, and the half of the hive that decided to swarm. After thirty minutes, they left. I was sure then that what I had just experienced was indeed a swarm.

Days before the swarm, the hive becomes excitable and the bees eat honey to prepare for their flight in order to be nourished and have provisions while they take time to build honeycomb in a new hive. When bees swarm, the worker bees stop feeding the queen and the queen tapers off egg-laying in order to lose weight to be able to fly. The worker bees are also responsible for creating queen cells by feeding larva bees some milk, royal jelly (instead of pollen), and honey. The creation of new queen cells ensures the survival of the hive after the preexisting queen has left with the swarm. The hive sends out scouts to find a new location for the hive to build and begin its colony.

When it is time to swarm, the workers push the queen down to the hive entrance and the queen will try to make her way back up in the hive. When the queen doesn't leave the hive, which is what happened to my hive the first time I saw them fill up the sky, they return to the hive. The bees who are planning to leave the hive will wait and try again another day. When a hive has limited space, the bees understand the colony is at risk—limited space means limited resources—and the bees prepare to swarm, thus reproducing the colony. A single colony becomes two, ensuring the survival and continuation of the hive.

This brings us back to the practice we could learn so much about: seeing ourselves as a whole hive and doing everything in service of the hive because of one's devotion to the hive. Generation upon generation of beings supporting the hive and larger ecosystem in which we exist, creating a process by which humanity and collective care for one another continues for infinity. What would it be like for us to embody a responsibility for our collective hive? What would it be like to create spaces for us to grieve what has been lost as a result of our forgetting that we are interconnected and part of a fragile and beautiful ecosystem, shared and composed of sentient beings whose survival is as important as our own? How might we begin to break down systems that separate us from remembering we are part of a hive and that we have different roles to ensure our collective liberation and survival? What would it feel like to be devoted to the liberation of all?

PRACTICE
Remembering Our True Nature

The following practice focuses on our true nature, one that is interconnected with and interdependent to all other sentient beings and the planet.

As part of your preparation, please meditate on or journal about the following questions:

- What are you grieving as a result of the knowledge that many have forgotten we are a hive, interconnected and interdependent?
- What would support you in remembering your interconnectedness with all sentient beings and the planet?

- What unique role can you embody in the hive in service of our shared humanity?

Take some time and work with these questions for as long as you would like.

PRACTICE
Bhramari

Find a comfortable way to be in your body.

Take a few moments to settle and center.

Connect with your inhales and exhales, and take a moment to breathe.

Feel the breath fill up the lungs and then empty.

Now, find a way to connect with your core and heart. You can place a hand on your belly, a hand on your heart, or simply bring your awareness to those energy centers in the body.

Take a moment to feel your hands rise and fall with each cycle of breath.

As you connect with your belly/core, realign with the value of interconnectedness and interdependence. Bring other beings who you love and care for into your awareness.

Spend a moment here.

Now begin to engage *bhramari*, or bumblebee's breath. You begin by withdrawing your senses. You can do this by closing your eyes and turning inward, or by moving into a hand mudra where you cover your eyes with your hands. A different version of the mudra has you place your thumbs in your ears, pinkies on the corners of your lips, third fingers at the base of your nostrils, middle fingers over your eyelids, and index fingers around your third eye at the center of your forehead, between your eyebrows.

Choose your hand position and take a deep breath in and out. Inhale, and with your next exhale, make a buzzing sound with your lips closed. It will sound similar to the buzzing of a bee. Repeat this six times. Each time you buzz, become aware of the collective buzz, the other beings in our ecosystem who hold a deep and real connection with you.

Release the hand mudra and take a moment to notice how you feel.

When you are ready, repeat the following mantra three times:

> I feel the buzz in my spirit.
> I feel the spirit of others in my spirit.
> I feel the whole hive.
> I am a powerful and necessary extension of the hive.
> I do everything I do in service of the collective hive.

I do not understand the mystery of grace—only that it meets us where we are and does not leave us where it found us.

—Anne Lamott, *Traveling Mercies*

THE TAPROOT

I was sitting in the chair next to the window that overlooked my garden as I spoke to her. Her voice was soothing, and I could tell she was listening intently. I could feel the care coming through her voice. At that time, I was a seasoned therapist myself and I was living in a small town, which meant it was very difficult to find a therapist I didn't know, have a professional relationship with, or who didn't know folks within my circle of friends. I called Mignon on a Saturday morning after a visit to the local farmers market.

We were in the heat of summer in North Carolina and the world was also feeling the heat in the aftermath of the acquittal of George Zimmerman, who was found innocent for the murder of Trayvon Martin. It was also the aftermath of Eric Garner, who was choked to death by a police officer in New York City; Michael Brown, who was murdered by a police officer in Ferguson, Missouri; Tamir Rice, who was murdered by a police officer in Cleveland, Ohio; Walter Scott, who was murdered by a police officer in Charleston, South Carolina; and Sandra Bland, who was found hanging in her jail cell in Walter County, Texas, after having been stopped for a minor traffic violation. It was the aftermath of so many more losses as a result of white supremacy experiencing Blackness as an atrocity.

Every time I would pass a police officer, my nervous system would go into fight, flight, or freeze; I felt terrified and like a moving target. Being Black was a risk factor for premature death. These losses didn't feel like death by a thousand cuts—they weren't microaggressions. Instead, they felt like death by a thousand gouges in my core and heart. Each time another Black person was murdered or taken from us because of white supremacy, it felt like some part of my soul and spirit was dying. I sought out a therapist because I was sure the PTSD I was experiencing was affecting every part of my existence—my relationships, my work, and my quality of life. I knew I needed help. The grief in response to those moments in our history threatened to swallow me whole.

In speaking with Mignon on the phone, I could tell she understood. I tried to explain all the grief held within my heart. Before I could get the words out of my mouth, she said, "I understand. I hear you." I knew she did. I went into her office and sat anxiously in her waiting room. Some of my anxiety emanated from the fact I had passed a police car on the highway en route to her office. When I would see a police officer on the road, I would grip the steering wheel a bit tighter and make sure I was going under the speed limit.

In addition to the police car dysregulating my nervous system, I was always a bit apprehensive when meeting a new therapist because I was a practicing clinical social worker at the time, and sometimes therapists make the worst clients. In the past, it has been difficult to let my guard down with therapists in a mental health system that has pathologized Black people without recognizing racial trauma as a lived experience most BIPOC experience. I had encountered so many therapists who didn't understand how racial trauma manifested, stemming from the white supremacist culture.

I was hopeful this experience would be different because of how compassionate and present Mignon had been during our initial phone consultation. She came out to get me from the waiting room and she did a standard intake session. Mignon was a Black woman, which I knew prior to meeting her because I searched on the Internet to learn more about her before we first met. She asked about my background, my work, what was bringing me into the space, and the standard questions about depression, anxiety, and suicidal ideation. Most of what I shared centered on PTSD and systemic racism, and the trauma of living within a racist culture while also working to dismantle white supremacy and racism. We also spent a fair amount of time talking about my relationship with my then-husband, Jeff, which was going through a major transition in large part due to changes I wanted to make that I didn't fully understand at the time. Even though I was choosing to shift our relationship, it was compounded by my PTSD and the concussion I had suffered after slipping on ice, nine months prior to meeting Mignon.

It was all connected, and it was difficult to tease apart—the trauma of white supremacy made my PTSD worse, the head injury made my depression intensify, and I was withdrawing from my relationships, friends, and community. We are complex beings, and the ways we feel dysregulated because of trauma usually stem from various experiences, not just one.

After my first session with Mignon, I felt a little more settled and confident she was the right fit for me in my pursuit to heal. The first session felt like a salve, which is what my nervous system so desperately needed. I continued to go back again and again. Over the course of eighteen months of therapy, my symptoms of PTSD began to decrease. My relationships were still in transition and evolving, and I was still a bit withdrawn from friends and community. I continued to have post-concussive syndrome, which was aggravating, but Mignon suggested some meditations and spiritually based tools to support my healing process specific to that injury.

Mignon was dynamic, authentic, and brought in many different healing techniques to address the various issues I was wading through. She validated me in a way that never before happened in other therapeutic relationships. She affirmed the depth of my intuition, and she understood synchronicity. She honored the divination tools I used for healing, and she led me to a place of contemplating what my daily ritual and practice would be. This practice came out of a moment of great crisis, which Mignon was shepherding me through. She knew I was a yoga practitioner and deeply spiritual, and she urged me to go deeper into my spiritual practice. She knew practice could help me respond to the deep despair I felt as a result of my own personal traumas and the traumas being experienced in the world. For the first time with consistency and dedication, I began to meditate every morning, pull divination cards, journal, write gratitude statements, and engage in other work focused on my higher purpose.

This daily practice led me to understand the level of grief I was attempting to move through, as well as the joy and resilience I was seeking. I felt like a construction site. Things were being moved around inside me as a result of my work with Mignon and my higher self. It was not gentle to be under construction in this way; it was necessary, but it felt as if I was being cracked open so that what needed to be revealed could come through me and out into the world. This is the kind of healing that happens when one truly allows the wound to open fully—to be exposed and raw, and for the pain to surface. It was a transformational experience.

Mignon witnessed this transformation. One day she looked at me and said, "You are a taproot." Intrigued and not knowing what else she would say, I listened intently. She went on to say, "The taproot extends downward and is the central line, the most dominant root from which all other roots sprout." Her words struck me. I had never heard anyone describe me as a root of any kind, but I knew I came from roots, ancestors, and a lineage made up of warriors, justice seekers, truth-tellers, and catalysts for change. Mignon's words stirred in my consciousness, alongside a few other axioms I had heard in the past from other healers I had sought out. "You came into this world to speed us up, to help us understand the urgency of what is happening." These were words I heard from a psychic in our first meeting. She was describing my birth and life's purpose. "If there is a crack in it, Michelle, you will expose it," were words a shaman once shared with me.

These beliefs were expressed about me by others who centralized my healing, and they all came together when Mignon shared with me about taproots. These archetypes—taproot, firestarter, catalyst, and revealer of what needs to be exposed—all lit a fire in my soul. Each of these archetypes spoke to my ability to be with the gravity of what we are losing collectively due to systems of oppression, cultural conditioning, and patterns that we must work to dismantle; to my capacity to grieve and encourage others to make space for their grief. These archetypes represent some of the greatest gifts I embody: my ability to influence, change, shift, reveal, inspire, and remember—which are practices connected to honoring our collective experience of grief and loss to create conditions for healing and liberation.

Mignon witnessed my process unfolding, and she supported me by offering tools to reground when things unsettled me. She affirmed me as our process unfolded. I did not have to justify my experience of trauma, racism, or even the head injury I was working to heal; therapy with her was truly a space where she just knew and understood all the words I shared with her. She was like a buoy, an energy, that uplifted me and made sure I stayed afloat. She guided me while I did the work of uncovering many truths about myself. She honored the deep trauma housed inside me that resulted from white supremacy and a culture that had conditioned so many to avoid and turn away from systems causing harm to us all. In her special way of revealing truths and bringing her medicine forth, she shared another statement with me connected to my archetype of a taproot, and this statement encapsulated what it is to grieve as an expression of being rooted in wanting oneself and others to be completely free. She said, "You must remember to remember. Remember who you are. Remember where you are from. Remember your wholeness. Remember."

This adage sang to my spirit of all the things we need to remember. To remember the historical wounds we are riddled with. The reality that if we don't heal, we risk causing more trauma. Grief is an experience that deserves to be witnessed and affirmed. We are nature. And knowing that, we need to create different and sustainable ways of living that center our humanity and the divinity and magic in all sentient beings and the natural world. When we "remember to remember" how we came to be in this moment when we are experiencing massive amounts of loss and grieving things we never imagined having to grieve, there is a space for us to allow our collective wounds to heal.

I have repeated "remember to remember" as a way of reminding myself and others that we know what is true. We know we are divine beings. We remember spiritual practice is medicine and an anchor for our own healing and the collective healing of us all. We know dominant culture tries to strip away our humanity. We know our own patterned behavior of stripping others' humanity away from them is a deeply damaging pattern, and we know we are being harmed by engaging in our toxic patterns. We know the cost of not grieving. We know dominant culture has stolen our rituals and ceremonies around grief through cultural appropriation and a desire to force us to move *past* instead of *through* grief. We have witnessed history repeat itself time and time again, and this dynamic is breaking our hearts. We want something different and better for us all. We know we have gifts and medicine that only we can bring forth. We know we are interconnected and bound. We understand we are precious to one another. We know dominant culture works to make us forget, and forgetting squelches our creativity and genius. We witness ourselves searching for refuge to heal our hearts.

Throughout *Finding Refuge*, you have moved through a journey of learning more about the grief that resides in your consciousness and bones. The grief that is held within our collective DNA. You have practiced, reflected, and hopefully communed with and moved through grief. You have made space to honor individual and collective grief. You have been offered practices to respond to your brokenheartedness and to open your heart. You have been guided back into wholeness and connected to your intuition and ancestors as a way of considering your right role and response to the cultural trauma that causes suffering and grief. You have been urged to remember the hive mind and the truth that our collective grief, trauma, and liberation are bound.

My hope is that your journey through *Finding Refuge* has reminded you of your own capacity to be a taproot, a catalyst, a person who is willing to look at what is exposed when cracks are revealed, and a person who centers healing the collective. From the experience of doing the heart work to heal your grief, your own medicine and what you can bring forth by honoring your grief has been revealed. Consider the medicine that moves through you—the offering you can now make to future generations as a lesson for them to honor their grief and interrupt systems and patterns that cause suffering.

Medicine is alchemical. Medicine is about transformation. As a collective, we must transform our relationship with grief to transform how we heal as a culture and collective. It is important to think of oneself as a medicine maker, because each one of us has a gift to offer the collective. And, our own individual stories of trauma, grief, and heartbreak aren't separate—they are interconnected, and they have equipped us with scars and wounds that can lead us to heal and break the patterns of trauma that perpetuate collective grief. If we do not process our grief now, it will stay in our bones and be passed on to future generations. Our wounds and scars will not heal but remain open. It is up to us to share lessons learned from doing this heart work, and the lessons that emerge while finding refuge in allowing grief to move through us, with future generations.

As you work to identify your particular medicine, here are some guiding questions for you:

- What have I learned about prioritizing my own grieving process?
- What do I know now that I didn't know when I began the journey of allowing grief to move through me?
- How can I center grief as a way of healing in the spaces in which I move?
- What have I learned about my own resilience?
- What have I learned about my ability to heal?
- What transformation is being called for at this time?
- What medicine can I bring forth that is not only my medicine but also rooted in the whole and all that is being offered to heal our collective?
- How might I inspire future generations to make space for their grief and responsibility to create conditions for liberation?

After you have had some time to reflect on these questions about your medicine and specific alchemy, please move through the guided practice below to contemplate what gifts you want to offer to future generations—gifts that will invite prioritizing and moving through collective grief, creating conditions for liberation for all.

PRACTICE
Tap the Root

At the beginning of your journey with *Finding Refuge*, you were guided to find an object to represent what was breaking your heart at the time. For this practice, please reconnect with your object. You can place it on an altar, near you on a table, or if you are sitting, on the ground around you. You will want its resonance with you for this practice. In addition to your object, and if they are accessible, please fill a clear vessel with water and a flowerpot or vessel with drainage with some dirt from your land. You will need enough dirt to fill the vessel. You will also need a seed of some kind. If you do not have a seed, you can still move through this practice. You can work with the elements of it and imagine using the seed when you get to that point in the practice. You will need a few small pieces of paper and a pen—paper you can fit into your vessel with dirt.

Set up your space with your object, the water, your seed, and your vessel with dirt. Place your pen and paper near you.

You will ground the body before working with the objects connected with this practice.

Find a comfortable seat, or if you prefer, you can stand or lie down. You might want to elevate your hips by sitting on a cushion or pillow, or a blanket.

Close your eyes or soften your gaze to the ground in front of you, and begin to breathe into your body. Start by taking deep breaths in and out. Begin to feel the shape change in your body as you breathe in and out. Notice the expansion as you breathe in, and the contraction or release with your exhale. Begin to notice the upward energy as you inhale and the downward energy as you exhale.

Breathe deeply into your body, noticing the physical sensations and emotions. Notice any spaces of tension or resistance, and respond to them with a deeper breath.

Bring your awareness to your solar plexus, which is above your belly button and below the sternum. The solar plexus is one of the energy centers in the body and it is associated with confidence, self-esteem, will, and determination. It is the energy center that precedes the heart. Yellow is the color associated with the solar plexus. Yellow, like the sun—a light shining brightly. Breathe into your solar plexus and imagine an orb of yellow light rooted there. The orb of light is pulsing with energy.

Now bring your awareness to the medicine you identified being able to bring forth. Imagine connecting your medicine with the yellow orb of light, and notice what happens. What is the alchemical reaction between your solar plexus, the yellow light, and your medicine? Stay here for as long as you would like, and when it is time to move out of the meditation, please take a moment to journal about your experience.

Now, locate your clear vessel of water and take a moment to connect with it. Notice the vessel, the qualities it embodies, and the water housed inside it. Imagine rooting your medicine in the water. Imagine a taproot extending down and other roots coming off the taproot. Imagine the water stimulating the growth of these roots. Now take a moment to consider what you wish for the roots that are extending from the taproot to embody. What do you want these new roots to know, share, or reveal about our collective grief and our capacity to heal?

- Do you want these new roots, which represent future generations, to understand it is imperative to make space for feelings and grief?
- Do you want them to understand how deeply connected we are to one another, sentient beings, and the natural world?
- Do you want these roots to grow into energies that recognize their responsibility to make cultural shifts that will decrease the presence and impact of cultural trauma?
- Do you want these new roots to grow with an awareness of the taproot and the space from which they sprouted?

- Do you want these roots to understand we can break down systems if we acknowledge the harmful impact of them?
- Do you want these roots to grow in ways that align with their intuition, deep-knowing, and the reality that we are nature?

Take a moment to be with these questions, the roots, and the water. When you feel ready, on the little pieces of paper, write down words that represent what you want the roots sprouting from the taproots to grow, be, inspire, reveal, and change. Then place the pieces of paper in the vessel with dirt, along with your seed, and pour the water over the seed, dirt, and papers that represent the roots that will sprout from your intentions.

Water the seed and watch it grow. If it would feel nourishing to you to write about the progress and growth, I invite you to do so.

From taproots come generative energy, growth, depth, nourishment, remembering, and connection. Remember that medicine is brimming in your bones as you engage in the heart work to heal our collective grief.

EPILOGUE

The process of writing *Finding Refuge* was like a shamanic journey. A journey where one travels to the past, seeking information, ancestral knowledge, and a connection with Spirit and one's higher self to move forward. Often shamanic journeys are accompanied by the rhythm of a drum mirroring the rhythm of a heartbeat. The heartbeat in this journey came from invoking the energies, ancestors, and practices shared in each chapter. The process of writing each chapter was vastly different. At times, I would feel joyous, and at other times, I felt as if I was slogging through body and heart memories of deep-seated grief.

My mother, Clara, was hospitalized on December 23, 2019, after I had already written the chapter about our process of navigating the medical system from her previous hospitalizations in the spring and summer of 2019. I was writing about her while I continued to fight for her humanity to be respected by the healthcare system. I wrote about the importance of practice and sadhana, sharing my own story of being stopped by a police officer weeks after Breonna Taylor was shot and killed in her home by police officers.

The exploration of wholeness in chapter 3 came from revisiting my father's energy and the trauma that made him feel broken to his core.

Eric urged me to build an altar and then move the altar outside and build a fire as I wrote about his life, intuition, and a connection with the natural world.

My grandmother invited me to place her ushering gloves on the altar I had built for her. I burned a candle made of wax from some of her candles as I wrote about her presence from the spirit realm in my life.

For the first time, I harvested honey from Sting a week after completing chapter 6. It is the best honey I have ever tasted.

As I thought about being a taproot and what readers might want to root for for future generations in chapter 7, my garden offered me fresh tomatoes, cucumbers, zucchini, and the largest and most beautiful sunflowers I have ever grown.

It was indeed a journey to transition *Finding Refuge* from idea to seed to sprout to completion. And throughout it, I went through my layers of grief while holding deep reverence for the experiences shared about my own losses and how they are linked to themes of loss within our collective experience.

I conceptualized the idea of a book about collective grief almost two years ago. At that time, I was beginning to notice a theme in my workshops and healing sessions—most people longed for a space to grieve. People wanted to grieve in response to systemic oppression and the pain they felt in response to their awareness that something needed to shift about the way we are living. People wanted a space to grieve all the ways we live unsustainably. A space to grieve for the planet. People needed space to grieve relationships lost due to different belief systems, paradigms, and lived experiences. People wanted to express grief related to how they were implicated in systems such as white supremacy, patriarchy, ableism, and classism. People most harmed by these systems needed a space to grieve the pain tethered to what it means to be othered by dominant culture.

This noticing made me begin to talk about my work as grief work whether it be in a Dismantling Racism workshop, a *Skill in Action* training, or an intuitive healing or therapy session.

The other awareness that emerged from claiming my work as grief work was the awareness that people have been deeply deprived of space to grieve their own individual losses let alone our collective losses. This would show up in a workshop setting when someone would cry about the tragic and horrific things of the day and then apologize for their tears. People would share about sadness, anger, frustration, and confusion, while not naming grief when all these emotional states are connected to what one experiences after they lose someone or something. People would intellectualize the content that was being presented about racism and white supremacy in an effort not to feel the emotions stirring inside them. They would stay in their heads and not their hearts, where I am sure their grief was housed.

People in my workshops didn't have a framework or language to describe their emotional responses as grief because, culturally, grief has been largely associated with the loss of a loved one. Grief has been seen as an individualized experience to be dealt with behind closed doors and in isolation. Like me, for some, grief arises physically first. People may reach out to health-care professionals to support them and be offered treatment for the physical body instead of responding to the heartbreak that is causing someone to grieve. In the system of mental health, depending on your proximity to power, your grief may be validated or made invisible. The traditional tools offered to people to move through grief have been talk therapy, medication, and support groups. These can be helpful tools. And other tools can support us in acknowledging and moving through our grief: spiritual practice, divination tools, connecting with the natural world, meditation, ceremony, and rituals.

Grieving has been underappreciated as a process that we all will encounter multiple times in our lifetimes. When space is made for people to center their grief and heartbreak, often it is time-limited, as if grieving has a beginning and an end point. It doesn't; it simply morphs as time goes on and is certainly not a linear or predictable experience. Our models for responding to grief have been based on the five stages of grief developed by Elisabeth Kübler-Ross: denial, anger, bargaining, depression, and acceptance. These stages do reflect some of what most people experience in response to loss, but they do not encapsulate what every individual experiences as they grieve in the wake of loss. The stages do not speak to how communities experience grief collectively and differently based on the identities individuals embody, nor do these stages acknowledge communities' history, ancestral trauma, racial trauma, or their continued exposure to the systems that may be causing grief and suffering by oppressing them.

Groups of people are pathologized for expressing their rage about the oppression they have had to endure for centuries. Their grief is almost never acknowledged. Instead, their humanity is questioned—dominant culture perpetuates the idea that people grieving in community and demanding justice are savage and destructive. Centuries of trauma, disappointment, and unattended heartbreak cause people to feel enraged and despaired. I believe communities are modeling new ways for us to grieve—out loud, in the open, and in community.

Although I conceptualized this book two years ago because I knew there was a need to normalize a conversation about cultural trauma and collective grief, I had no idea I'd be writing *Finding Refuge* amid COVID-19 and a resurgence of the Black Lives Matter movement. I didn't know confederate statues would be coming down, schools would be in the process of being renamed as a way of confronting white supremacy, or that we would constantly be wearing masks and using hand sanitizer while learning how to connect in new ways as we socially isolate ourselves. My entire writing process for *Finding Refuge* has occurred during the reign of COVID-19 as well as horrid displays of white supremacy, transphobia, capitalism, and a lack of attention to the collective care of all.

In March, when positive cases of COVID-19 began to emerge in the United States, I was preparing to travel to Canada and the Pacific Northwest. I contemplated what it meant to not show up to teach, and I ultimately decided I needed to stay put in North Carolina as an act of both protecting myself from contracting the virus and protecting others because of its contagious nature. At the time of my writing these words, the virus has persisted for several months. As it has progressed and taken hold of our lives in a way many of us have never experienced, hospitals have been overrun with patients as they lack the appropriate supplies to protect the health-care workers who are caring for those who are sick;

health centers haven't had enough testing kits, and people have been dying, and dying alone.

As of November 2, 2020, 9.28 million people in the United States and 46.6 million people worldwide have contracted COVID-19. In the United States, 231,000 people have died from COVID-19 and 1.2 million worldwide. The numbers continue to rise daily and as we approach flu season and the cold of winter in the Western Hemisphere, there are reports of record breaking numbers of new cases each day as well as news of the unfathomable number of deaths from COVID-19. Families have been unable to be with their loved ones as they transition out of their physical bodies, and at best have been able to Zoom or call into hospital rooms and skilled nursing facilities to say goodbye. People are holding funerals on Zoom, which has become the platform and lifeline for connection. Scientists theorized the number of positive cases would decrease in the heat of summer—the opposite has occurred. People are still demanding the economy stay open, that children return to school, that college students go back to universities and dorm rooms, that restaurants and bars stay open, and for all intents and purposes that we act as if things were normal before and are normal now.

As COVID-19 has ravaged our lives in ways we could not have imagined, we are reconfiguring our psychology and our way of being and connecting. Amid it all, the murder of Ahmaud Arbery, who was out for a jog in a predominantly white neighborhood, came to light. Breonna Taylor was murdered by the police as she slept in her bed. All of the police officers involved in the murder of Breonna were acquitted with the exception of Brett Hankison who was charged with "wantonly and blindly" shooting into Breonna's apartment. He was accused of endangering lives in the neighboring apartment unit not for taking Breonna's life.* George Floyd became a name chanted all over the globe in the call for Black Lives to Matter after Derek Chauvin, a former Minneapolis police officer, put his knee into George Floyd's neck for eight minutes and forty-six seconds, murdering him as George called for his mother and uttered the words Eric Garner uttered on December 30, 2017: "I cannot breathe."

Finding refuge became a practice I found myself needing while writing this book. The world is shifting in ways I have never experienced, and while there is hope, there is still deep heartbreak in response to the patterns we as a collective continue to repeat: denial, rewriting history, valuing some lives over others, and pretending things are normal when they are not. As I wrote *Finding Refuge*, I responded to my grief and the deep heartbreak and losses my spirit felt every time I read the latest data about deaths from COVID-19, and every time I watched another Black person's life expire because of whiteness. I wrote *Finding Refuge* as so many looked to me to hold space for their grief while I waded through my own soul-shaking despair. I wrote through my anger, frustration, and confusion in response to how we could ever act as if things could go back to "normal."

There was no way to write *Finding Refuge* without moving through the grief of my own individual experiences relating to loss, and there was no way to write *Finding Refuge* without feeling the collective losses we face in real time, right now—both the loss and grief to come in the aftermath of COVID-19, and the

---

* Mark Berman et al., "Officer Brett Hankison Charged with Wanton Endangerment; Two Officers Shot during Protests," *Washington Post*, September 24, 2020, https://www.washingtonpost.com/nation/2020/09/23/breonna-taylor -charging-decision/.

grief relating to the tentative hopefulness that Black Lives will begin to Matter.

Two years ago, in my bones, I knew a conversation about collective grief needed to be elevated and centered; I just didn't know what we would be grieving prior to my writing *Finding Refuge*. This process of being called to write and create something for collective healing isn't new for me. My process is to listen to the ancestors and Spirit, and to notice what is being called for in the collective and what I am being moved to offer at a particular time. I listen and then create in service of our collective healing.

I am quite sure I have my mother to thank for this process. She is the one who listened when Cassandra came to her and decided she would be an energy and deity in my life. When my mother was pregnant with me, she was in the grocery store and the name Cassandra came to her. I am convinced I was speaking to her through the womb. My mother shares the story as if she just heard the name and was curious about why, but she listened to the call similar to the way I listen when I am called to bring something from the spirit world into the material world. My mother had already decided that she wanted to name her children Michael and Michelle, and when Cassandra came to her, it became my middle name. For years, I thought my middle name was pretty but I didn't feel connected to it in a deep way. I felt like a Michelle, and I knew my last name Johnson wasn't mine—it was likely given to me through my ancestors' experience of being enslaved by a slave master with the namesake Johnson.

When I was in my early twenties, my relationship to my middle name shifted when a professor at UNC-Chapel Hill pointed it out and directed me toward the Greek mythology of Cassandra. I read about her and realized she was a prophetess, but was cursed.

People didn't believe her predictions. She predicted things like the Trojan War, sharing premonitions about the Trojan horse that wasn't a gift horse, but instead the demise of the Trojans. Her warnings were often disregarded and not believed due to her curse.

In my early forties, a friend, Asa, gifted me a book about Cassandra and told me the people Cassandra shared her predictions with could absolutely hear her. Asa went on to tell me, "They didn't want to hear Cassandra." Knowing the truth, sharing it, and being heard and not being listened to or being able to be heard are very different experiences. My hope is that throughout *Finding Refuge* you not only learned to listen more deeply to your inner-knowing, the truths you know, and the things you no longer want to pretend aren't real, but that you also heeded the invitation offered throughout the book—to grieve in order to heal and find liberation.

As the seed of the idea for *Finding Refuge* emerged, I knew it would grow and blossom at the right time. A time when we most needed it. As Cassandra, in collaboration with Spirit and my ancestors, was conjuring the idea for *Finding Refuge* and bringing it to life, she did so because she knew we would need the medicine and healing that can come from grieving together, in community. She knew we would be grieving in response to massive shifts in our global experience and consciousness.

The process of being with my own grief, and seeing and sitting with our collective grief has reaffirmed these beliefs: If we do not figure out how to acknowledge the reality that we are experiencing great losses, and if we do not find ways to witness each other as we grieve and hold the tenderness of being alive during a pandemic, civil unrest, systemic oppression, and climate change, we will continue to harm one another. If we stuff our tears down into our bodies, repressing what most needs to be expressed, we will die from broken hearts and unprocessed grief. We will continue to perpetuate systems that mimic COVID-19, systems that affect those most marginalized, those with less proximity to power. Systems that are designed to take the breath away.

We will stagnate instead of rising up as protestors in the streets, in our homes, and on social media.

We are being guided to rise up. There is a collective call for history to cease repeating itself, and instead to make reparations and valuing Black Lives an essential practice. We have an opportunity to reveal what most of us feel: deep heartbreak, resilience, and the desire to heal and come back into balance and wholeness, individually and collectively. We have an opportunity to heal. It is my hope that this offering and your own practice of finding refuge will give you what you need to heal, and that we will all heal.

May you be safe, happy, and free. May all beings everywhere be safe, happy, and free, and may our thoughts, words, and actions contribute to that safety, happiness, and freedom for all. May your grief be honored and seen. May our grief be honored and seen. May we expose and regurgitate what needs to be processed now so we do not pass on trauma to future generations. May we move through the loving act of being with our tender hearts and our grief. May we move through the loving act of being in space together, witnessing one another in our healing.

Àṣẹ, and so it is.

ABOUT THE AUTHOR

Michelle Cassandra Johnson is a social justice warrior, author, Dismantling Racism trainer, empath, yoga teacher and practitioner, and intuitive healer. With more than twenty years of experience leading Dismantling Racism workshops and working with clients as a licensed clinical social worker, she has a deep understanding of how trauma impacts the mind, body, spirit, and heart. Her awareness of the world through her own experience as a Black woman allows her to know, firsthand, how privilege and power operate.

Michelle has a bachelor of arts degree from the College of William and Mary and a master's degree in social work from the University of North Carolina-Chapel Hill. She has worked in several nonprofits and served as an elected official and on many nonprofit boards of directors. She has worked with large corporations, small nonprofits, and community groups, including the ACLU-WA, Duke University, Google, This American Life, the Center for Equity and Inclusion, Eno River Unitarian Universalist Church, Lululemon, and many others. Michelle published *Skill in Action: Radicalizing Your Yoga Practice to Create a Just World* in 2017 to great acclaim, and she teaches workshops in yoga studios and community spaces nationwide. She is on the faculty of Off the Mat, Into the

149

World. Michelle was a TEDx speaker at Wake Forest University in 2019, and she has been interviewed on several podcasts in which she explores the premise and foundation of *Skill in Action*, along with creating ritual in justice spaces, our divine connection with nature and Spirit, and how we as a culture can heal.

Michelle leads courageously from the heart with compassion and a commitment to address the heartbreak that dominant culture causes for many because of the harm it creates. She inspires change that allows people to stand in their humanity and wholeness in a world that fragments most of us. Whether in an anti-oppression training, a yoga space, or individual or group intuitive healing sessions, the heart, healing, and wholeness are at the center of how she approaches all her work in the world. She lives in Winston-Salem, North Carolina, with her sweet dog, Jasper, and her bees.